Stories I Need to Tell

Vol. 3

SCREENPLAYS BY DOUGLAS KING

DAY III
Productions
film • publishing • events

www.DayIIIProd.com

DAY
III
Productions
film • publishing • events

INTRODUCTION

I have been writing screenplays professionally for three decades. In that time, I have written scripts I am immensely proud of, and others that, well, let's just say, the fact they never saw the silver screen is probably a good thing for all parties concerned. I have written for major studios, independent studios, independent producers as well as my own spec scripts, some of which you hold in our hands now.

Screenplays by their very essence are just stories presented in a format that makes them accessible for other creative individuals (directors, costume designers, set designers and actors, to name a few) to produce a motion picture or television show. As most writers know, getting a spec screenplay sold and produced into a film is tantamount to winning the lottery. The odds may actually be better to win the lottery.

In light of this, and despite this, I have continued to write my screenplays for many reasons. First, I truly love the process and enjoy breaking story, developing character and plot and working out the story beats. Second, call me delusional, but there is an optimistic part of me that still believes these scripts may be sold and produced one day, which ultimately leads me to my final reason for what some might say is a sadomasochistic endeavor, I must tell these stories.

These stories, characters, settings and themes have burrowed themselves so deeply into my mind and psyche that if I do not release them onto the page, like a geothermal geyser, they would simply burst forth through the mantel of my mind causing who knows what type of irreparable damage.

What you hold in your hands is the product of many years of writing. Each volume in this series includes two spec screenplays of stories I have to tell. It has become a moral imperative that I release these stories to the public. And, if they are not made into the films they are meant to mature into, transitioning from a caterpillar to a beautiful butterfly, then at least they can be enjoyed in their pupa form within the pages of this book.

I hope you enjoy these stories. If you do and if you would like to see them metamorphosize into what they can be—a life action feature film—let me know. The best by-product of screenwriting is that it blooms into the collaborative art of filmmaking and storytelling.

These are the stories I need to tell. Maybe we can tell some together.

In this, the third volume of my *Stories I Need to Tell* series of screenplay compilations, the theme is faith and humanity in the form of two individuals and their struggle with mortality and living a life full of meaning. *Talk* is the story of a radio shock-jock who faces mortality while staging a marathon radio program where the topic is his own death. By facing death, our lead discovers the importance of living a balanced life.

While there is no life and death crisis in *Art Life*—one man's journey of self-discovery through the art he creates—there is a crisis of faith. Faith in one's ability and talent. One man struggles to define who he is as an artist as he faces losing a life-long career and the people who love him.

Douglas King
February 2020

LOGLINE

When a radio shock-jock learns his decision to choose his career over treatment for throat cancer results in a fatal diagnosis, he stages an on-air marathon where he faces his mortality while trying to forestall the worse event for a radio host, dead air.

TALK

by
Douglas King & William Phillips

INT. RADIO STUDIO

PARAMEDICS rush into the radio studio to tend to radio talk
show host NEWT RICHARDSON who has fallen on the floor.

The paramedics attempt to remove Newt's wife VERONICA from
the room, but CHARLES RILEY, the producer of Newt's program,
stops them.

Veronica holds Newt's hand. REED and LAURA watch in horror.

                         PARAMEDIC
               Clear!

The paramedic's shock Newt in an attempt to restart his
heart.

THE HEART MONITOR BEEPS and ALARMS as Newt is in cardiac
arrest.

Veronica cries.

A commotion in the room as the paramedics try to revive Newt.

The sound of the heart monitor acts as a SOUND BRIDGE TO:

INT. RADIO STUDIO

The mouth of the radio talk show host is less than an inch
from the microphone.

The voice of NEWT RICHARDSON is raspy and he pauses during
his tirade to cough a harsh, dry cough.

Newt is pale and gaunt.

                         NEWT
               Holy mother of everything sweet and
               pure in this world, this has been
               one of the strangest programs we
               have had in a while. The natives
               are restless today folks, so batten
               down the hatches, stow away your
               daughters and lock n' load in case
               the weirdness comes callin' on your
               doorstep. I'll tell you people,
               sometimes you scare me. There are a
               lot of things that scare me. Bill
               Clinton having won two elections
               scares me. Jon Goselin becoming
               famous scares me spitless.
                         (MORE)

NEWT (CONT'D)

> But today, you people, my faithful
> audience, you have scared me beyond
> all natural fear.

INTERCUT: NEWT'S VO PLAYS FROM THE RADIO OVER THIS SERIES OF
SHOTS

INT. CAR - MORNING

A BUSINESS MAN sits in his car during rush hour traffic.

INT. OFFICE - MORNING

A SECRETARY listens to Newt's show on Internet radio in her
cubicle at work.

EXT. CONSTRUCTION SITE - MORNING

A group of CONSTRUCTION WORKERS listen to Newt on a small
radio they have set up near where they are working.

EXT. JOG PATH - MORNING

A male JOGGER listens to the radio via a headset.

BACK TO SCENE

NEWT (CONT'D)

> I will stay awake at night,
> quivering under my covers,
> wondering what thoughts are
> creeping through your festering
> brain pans, and I take no comfort
> in knowing that you will all return
> to me tomorrow morning. But hey, we
> deserve each other right? You scare
> me. I probably scare a lot of you.
> I even scare myself sometimes, but
> only because I amaze myself. I
> mean, you get as good as me and it
> would scare you too. Well people,
> that's it for another day. Be good
> to one another, love your neighbor,
> don't covet your neighbor, and
> don't kill your neighbor.

The CLOSING THEME SONG PLAYS.

Newt takes off his headphones and sits still for a minute as if he is unsure whether to get up or not.

His assistant, LAURA, enters the studio. She hands Newt a cup of water.

> LAURA
> You don't look so well today, Newt.

> NEWT
> Really? You mean because I've lost fifteen pounds and my skin hangs off of me like dirty dishrags, I don't look like the picture of health? Kidding Laura. I'm fine.

> LAURA
> Maybe you should take tomorrow off?

> NEWT
> Trying to get rid of me? I'll tell you what, when I want to take a day off I'll let you know. Until then you can expect to see my withering butt sitting in this seat, making sunshine and happiness for all those radio listeners.

> LAURA
> That would certainly be a first

> NEWT
> (surprised)
> Good, good. I see my charm is finally wearing off on you. Glad to see you coming around with some cheek yourself. And speaking of cheek, you look very good in those jeans today. But enough sexual harassment for one morning, I must be off. See you tomorrow.

> LAURA
> If I must.

Newt smiles and leaves the studio

INT RADIO STATION HALLWAY - DAY

On his way out of the radio station, Newt is stopped by his producer, CHARLES RILEY. Charles is roughly the same age as Newt. More handsome and refined. Whereas Newt wears jeans and slogan T-shirts, Charles is business casual.

Along the walls of the station halls hang promotional posters for Newt and his various stunts, or live events.

> CHARLES
> Hey Newt, good show today.

> NEWT
> Well, well Mr. Office-boy coming
> down to smooze with the worker
> bees. How's the oxygen upstairs?

> CHARLES
> You never give it a rest do you?

> NEWT
> You don't pay me enough to be able
> to take a rest. So what brings you
> down to the dungeons?

> CHARLES
> I wanted to discuss tomorrow's bit.

> NEWT
> what's to discuss?

> CHARLES
> You are riding the edge of good
> taste and decency.

> NEWT
> Man, have you lost grip with that
> makes good radio? Do you even
> remember what it feels like to have
> balls? I thought you knew that
> irritating people was what life was
> all about.

> CHARLES
> I'll take your word for it.

> NEWT
> Let's get people riled up so we can
> have some dynamic conversation.

> CHARLES
> Confrontation is more likely.

> NEWT
> Even better.

> CHARLES
> If that's the way you want to play
> it, I'll support it. But under
> protest.

                    NEWT
          Dully noted and ignored. Anything
          else?

                    CHARLES
          I know I've asked you this on
          Monday, but are you feeling well?
          To be frank, you look terrible.

                    NEWT
          Thank you Charles, I can always
          count on your tact and honesty.
          I've just been putting in a lot of
          hours lately. I'm feeling fine,
          thank you. A little thinner and
          paler maybe, but all in all no
          worse for the wear.

                    CHARLES
          Well, whether you believe it or
          not, I worry about you.

                    NEWT
          I appreciate the concern and, trust
          me, nobody is more worried about
          me, than myself. If we're finished,
          I will bid you farewell until
          tomorrow.

                    CHARLES
          Yeah, we're done. I will see you in
          the morning.

INT. DOCTOR'S OFFICE - LATER

Newt sits in a well appointed doctor's office.

Nervous, he fidgets while he waits for the doctor.

DOCTOR TOMKINS enters from a doorway behind Newt carrying a
folder.

                    NEWT
          Doc, you wouldn't leave a dying man
          waiting would you? I mean, what if
          I died before I could pay your
          bill? So what's the word?

                    DOCTOR TOMKINS
          Not good, Newt. As I told you when
          we first found out about the
          cancer, if it went untreated it was
          only going to get worse and I was
          right, it has.

                    NEWT
          How bad is it?

                    DOCTOR TOMKINS
          The mass in your throat and
          esophagus has enlarged, as I'm sure
          you have probably been able to
          notice on your own. That in itself
          is not good, but even worse is that
          the biopsy has revealed that it's
          spread to your lymph nodes and
          lungs as I feared. There is no
          telling without further tests just
          how far it has spread through your
          body. My guess is that you are full
          of it.

                    NEWT
          Yeah, but what about the cancer?

                    DOCTOR TOMKINS
          It is killing you, Newt.

                    NEWT
          Don't you find it interesting that
          I would get throat cancer,
          considering most people think I
          talk out of my ass.

                    DOCTOR TOMKINS
          By not letting me treat you for the
          past year, you have certainly
          proven that you are one.

                    NEWT
          Good one, Doc. I'll remember that
          when I'm writing my Will.

                    DOCTOR TOMKINS
          Newt, do you understand what I am
          telling you?

                    NEWT
               (faux seriousness)
          Yes Doctor. You are telling me I am
          going to die. Is that about right?

                    DOCTOR TOMKINS
          I don't understand why you didn't
          let me treat you when we could have
          maybe stopped this.

                    NEWT
          It was that "maybe," Doc. Maybe you
          could have stopped it, maybe not.
          Maybe I would have just lost my
          voice. I've explained that to you a
          million times. I'm not about to let
          you hack around my throat and run
          the risk of losing my voice and my
          career. I've spent my whole life
          building a career around my voice
          and I'm not willing to live talking
          through a voice box.

                    DOCTOR TOMKINS
          Well, by making that decision
          you've lowered your chances of
          surviving this.

                    NEWT
          So, how much time do I have left?

                    DOCTOR TOMKINS
          Newt, in my professional opinion, I
          give you less then a month to live.
          I suggest, if you haven't already,
          you and Veronica begin putting your
          affairs in order.

INT. DINING ROOM - NIGHT

Newt sits at a dinner table with VERONICA, a lovely woman who
has aged well in spite of being married to Newt. A small gold
cross hangs from a modest chain around her neck.

Their home is nicely decorated and furnished.

Eating and swallowing are difficult and painful for Newt.

Newt clears his throat.

                    NEWT
          I saw Doctor Tomkins today,

Veronica, noticeably shaken when she hears Tomkins' name,
puts her fork down.

                    VERONICA
You didn't tell me you had an
appointment

                    NEWT
I didn't want you worrying.

                    VERONICA
     (sarcastically)
How so very like you.
     (beat)
     (softer and more serious)
So is everything okay?

                    NEWT
     (flippantly)
Well, he gives me a month to live.

                    VERONICA
You're joking.

                    NEWT
No.

                    VERONICA
Newt!

                    NEWT
It seems that the cancer has spread
and become much worse. We knew this
day would come. It was just a
matter of time and unfortunately my
time is now.

                    VERONICA
How could you not have told me
things were getting this bad?

                    NEWT
I didn't want you to overreact.

                    VERONICA
Overreact! You treat me like a five-
year-old. Give me a little respect
before you assume I won't be able
to handle some news.

                    NEWT
But this is exactly how I knew you
would react.

                    VERONICA
I'm reacting to your insensitivity.
Don't you think I deserve to know?

Veronica is even more emotional now.

>   VERONICA (CONT'D)
>   Well, we better get some other
>   opinions. You can start radiation
>   of chemo. Maybe we can stop this.

>   NEWT
>   It's too late Veronica. Besides, if
>   I wanted to prolong my death I'd
>   have gotten treated a year ago.
>   We've been through this. The risk…

Veronica cries. Pushes her play away.

Newt takes a few more bites of his dinner.

>   VERONICA
>   What risk? The risk of living?

>   NEWT
>   You know how I feel about those
>   treatments. And don't get me
>   started on doctors. They're all a
>   bunch of heartless boobs who took
>   up their profession to make money,
>   play golf and work as little as
>   possible. It certainly was not to
>   heal people. Besides, how would I
>   look bald? Pro basketball players
>   are the only celebrities that can
>   get away with…

>   VERONICA
>   Newt, you're on the radio, who
>   would have ever seen you, you fool!

>   NEWT
>   Now we resort to name calling? Have
>   some compassion, I'm dying here.

Veronica slaps Newt and leaves the room.

Newt follows her after eating one more bite of his dinner.

INT. LIVING ROOM

Veronica sits on the couch crying. She hugs a pillow tightly
to her chest.

Newt comes up to her and puts his arms around her.

The two hug.

                    NEWT
          Honey, I love you. But radio is all
          I have ever wanted to do. The risk
          of losing my voice and living was
          far worse for me than dying.

                    VERONICA
          What about me? Did you ever once
          stop to consider what I wanted.
          Maybe having you speechless and
          live was better than speechless and
          dead?

                    NEWT
          I'm not sure if that is a
          compliment or not.

                    VERONICA
          Newt, you never took my feelings
          into consideration.

                    NEWT
          I didn't want to feel sick all the
          time, or be tethered to the
          hospital. I wanted to be able to
          spend my last days with you doing
          whatever, and going wherever, we
          wanted to. I just wanted to spend
          my time with you and not a bunch of
          doctors.

                    VERONICA
          But we didn't even do that! You
          spent all of your time on the
          radio!

Veronica, still crying, excuses herself and leaves the room.

INT. RADIO STATION, CHARLES' OFFICE - DAY

Newt meets with Charles and SHELLY JOHNSON, all business and
no play make Shelly a great advertising director.

                    SHELLY
          As you may have heard we have some
          major new national accounts joining
          us. It's important that we keep
          them satisfied.

                    CHARLES
          Hear, "not piss them off."

                    NEWT
          What were our ratings last week?
          That's all the advertisers should
          be worried about. How many ears are
          listening? I don't care who buys
          time on my show and they shouldn't
          care what I say.

                    SHELLY
          In a perfect world that's great. We
          need to set the limits of what you
          say. We don't want to offend
          anyone.

                    NEWT
          That's what I do best. Have you
          ever listen to my show?

                    SHELLY
          We're talking about millions of
          dollars

                    NEWT
          How many times have we had this
          conversation, Chuck? I don't care
          about the advertisers.

                    CHARLES
          Newt, all we want to do is ensure
          that there is no conflict.

                    NEWT
          Look, I guess I can't keep this a
          secret much longer, and seeing as
          we do work together for the same
          greater good and all...Well, I
          should tell you both. I'm dying.

Shelly startles at Newt's comment.

Charles reacts by not reacting.

                    CHARLES
          If this is your lame attempt to get
          out of this meeting it isn't going
          to work.

                    NEWT
          No such luck Chuck. I'll be dead
          soon. Very soon in fact, so I
          couldn't care less whether we
          offend anyone.

                    SHELLY
          Oh my...!

                    CHARLES
               (suspiciously)
          And what are you dying from?

                    NEWT
          I have cancer. It started about a
          year ago and just keeps spreading.
          Should be all the way to my big toe
          by now.

                    CHARLES
          Are you serious?

                    NEWT
          As a heart attack. (beat) Scratch
          that...as cancer.

                    CHARLES
          Newt, tell me you are kidding. Tell
          me this is another sick prank of
          yours.

                    NEWT
          Chuck, look at me. I've lost almost
          as much weight as Oprah put on this
          week. I look like a scarecrow that
          someone forgot to stuff with straw.
          I'm buying the farm big guy.
          Cashing the last check. Kicking the
          bucket. Going to the big dirt farm.

                    SHELLY
          Stop it. Just stop it.

                    CHARLES
          Shelly, why don't you excuse us for
          a minute.

Shelly leaves the office.

Newt reclines in his chair facing Charles.

Charles leans forward. Weighing the new information and
processing what it means.

                    CHARLES
          I can't believe you've known about
          this for a year and haven't told
          me.

                    NEWT
Last time I checked, I wasn't
married to you and you aren't my
mom. I didn't know I had to tell
you.

                    CHARLES
Newt! We have worked together for
twenty years and you treat me like
an outsider.

                    NEWT
Hey, you left the show for
Suitsville, not me.

                    CHARLES
Oh get off it! You know very well
if I didn't join the front office
your...both of our butts would have
been kicked off radio long ago.
This is how you show your
friendship, dropping this in my lap
as if I was some next door neighbor
you just happen to see while mowing
the lawn?

                    NEWT
Sorry, Chuck. I didn't think it was
that big of a deal. Besides, I
didn't want you nagging me to get
treatment.

                    CHARLES
You selfish son-of-a...! Don't you
think as your producer I have a
right to know if my talent is going
to make it in the next day or if
he'll be dead! And are you telling
me you could have had this treated?

                    NEWT
There was an procedure but I didn't
like the risk associated with it.
There was a possibility of me
losing my voice for good and I
wasn't willing to accept that.

                    CHARLES
So you opted to lose your life
instead? Brilliant decision-making,
Newt. Really got to hand it to you
on that call.

                    NEWT
Bite me! (beat) Do you really think
that pleases me? I was hoping to be
around to irritate you for a lot
longer. Speaking of which, I've
got a great idea! One that's never
been done before, and it will be
awesome. What if we did a marathon
program until I died? We could call
it the Countdown to Dead Air.
Basically, I will stay on the air
taking calls, running old bits and
the usual stuff until I take my
final breath. What do you think?

                    CHARLES
That is the sickest idea I have
ever heard.

                    NEWT
Yeah, but do you want to do it? Now
that would be unbelievable. Our
ratings would go through the roof.

                    CHARLES
You can't be serious?

                    NEWT
Oh I'm dead serious, pun intended.

                    CHARLES
Newt, what are you saying?

                    NEWT
I'm saying that I want to stay on
the air until I'm dead. It will be
my swan song. My coup de gras. My
curtain call. It will be the
greatest show ever.

                    CHARLES
You are serious. Newt, I'm not
finished being mad at you yet.
Don't change the subject. Anyway,
there is no way we can do that. Do
you honestly believe that the
station would allow you to die on
the air?

                    NEWT
Why not? Most of the stiffs in
suits upstairs think I die on the
air every day.

                    CHARLES
          You know what I mean.

                    NEWT
          I know that long time ago another
          Charles Riley would have loved this
          idea. But that was B.S. Before
          Suit. Look Chuck, I really want to
          do this and I know I need your
          help. Let's do this thing. Like the
          old days when we ran wild like
          jackals across the Serengeti.
          Consider it a dying man's last
          request.

INT. RESTAURANT - DAY

A fancy restaurant.

Newt eats a salad.

Veronica dabs the tears in her eyes then scowls at Newt.

                    VERONICA
          Oh Newt, how morbid.

                    NEWT
          No, it will be cool. Uplifting!
          Enlightening! See, I stay on the
          air until I finally pass away. Get
          it, Countdown to Dead Air?

                    VERONICA
          I get it. I just can't believe you
          are suggesting it. What does
          Charles think about this?

                    NEWT
          Ah, you know Chuck, he doesn't have
          a thought unless the other suits
          give it to him. But he said he
          would try to pass it by the station
          manager.

Veronica thinks about what Newt has proposed.

Newt sits anxiously waiting for her comment.

                    NEWT
          What do you think?

                    VERONICA
I think that...I can't believe,
even now, in your final days, you
would rather spend it on that radio
show than spending time with me and
taking care of yourself.

                    NEWT
You know I can't take care of
myself. I never was able to do
that, but this is the one thing I
am able to do well. The one thing I
love most in the world.

                    VERONICA
Obviously

                    NEWT
I mean other than you.

                    VERONICA
Come home and let me take care of
you.

                    NEWT
Honey, this is something I really
want to do.

                    VERONICA
There is always something you
really want to do and it always
comes before what I want. Newt, I
am not a priority in your life and
I never have been.

                    NEWT
That's not true.

                    VERONICA
Yes it is! That radio show has
always come before me. I have let
it go because I love you and I know
it means everything to you, but
this is going too far. To want to
spend your last days on Earth in
that studio is just plain sick.

                    NEWT
But, honey, I want your blessing on
this and I want you with me the
entire time.

                    VERONICA
          What if I don't give you my
          blessing? What then?

                    NEWT
          Then, I do the show without your
          blessing?

                    VERONICA
          So what does it matter if you have
          it or not? You're going to do
          whatever you want anyway, as usual.

                    NEWT
          Yes, but if I have your blessing it
          will mean so much to me.

                    VERONICA
          You're so full of it. I don't think
          you can tell when you're on air or
          off any longer. The B.S. just keeps
          rolling right along.

                    NEWT
          That's not fair.

                    VERONICA
          What you're asking of me isn't
          fair! You expect me to give you my
          blessing so you can spend the last
          hours I will ever see you alive
          talking with the nation. Well I'm
          sorry, Newt. I don't want to share
          those hours. Excuse me for being
          selfish for once, but I want to
          spend this time with you and you
          alone.

Veronica throws her napkin down on the table and exits
quickly, leaving Newt alone and a bit embarrassed.

INT. JOE FOSTER'S OFFICE - DAY

JOE FOSTER, the station manager, sits in his large and
impressive office.

The walls are adorned with photos of Joe with celebrities and
a few awards sit on the nearby bookshelf.

Charles and Newt sit across the desk from Joe.

Obviously uptight about being here Newt does not hide his
disdain for Joe well.

Similarly, Joe doesn't much care for Newt but puts up a good
front.

>   JOE FOSTER
>   First, let me say, Newt, how sorry
>   I am to hear about your condition.
>   Go over for me the details and
>   let's see if I understand
>   completely what you are proposing

>   NEWT
>   Basically, I am going to rant and
>   rave on the air for as long as I
>   can until I die. You will have the
>   first radio talk show host actually
>   to die on the radio.

>   JOE FOSTER
>   Not something I would be
>   necessarily proud of.

>   NEWT
>   Oh come on, Joe, let's cut the
>   crap. You've hated me and my type
>   of humor since you started here.
>   You only had to put up with me
>   because I was here long before you.
>   Look, I'm not going to butter you
>   up like Chuck would. I'm not very
>   good at that.

>   JOE FOSTER
>   Obviously.

>   NEWT
>   But, basically, I will do my show
>   as usual, only I will stay on the
>   air until I die. Think of the money
>   you will save by not having to pay
>   the other DJs for those days.

>   JOE FOSTER
>   That certainly isn't the point.

>   NEWT
>   Sure it is. Everything is about
>   money. Think of the publicity.
>   Think of the ratings. It's a sure-
>   fire winner.

>   JOE FOSTER
>   Charles, what do you think?

                    CHARLES
          If anyone can do it, Newt can. I've
          called many of our advertisers and
          they said they will stick with the
          show unless it gets morbid or
          grotesque.

                    JOE FOSTER
          Okay, Newt, here is what I will
          agree to right now—let me think
          more about it—but I want to give
          you an answer quickly. Promote the
          program, clear the schedule and go
          for it for one day. If the ratings
          are there, we don't lose any
          syndicates and the advertisers are
          still comfortable, we can go for a
          second day. But as soon as things
          get slow and it looks like the
          advertisers are pulling out, I'm
          pulling the plug.

                    NEWT
          Pun intended?

Charles shoots Newt a dirty look.

                    CHARLES
          That seems fair.

                    NEWT
          Whose definition of slow do we go
          by?

                    JOE FOSTER
          Newt, when will you ever be happy?
          I'm letting you do your show,
          against my better judgment, and
          still it's not enough for you. It's
          simple, if I start losing money,
          the show's off. That's the
          deal—take it or leave it.

                    CHARLES
          We'll take it.

Before Newt can say anything else.

                    CHARLES (CONT'D)
          Thanks for your time Joe, we
          appreciate it. Come on, Newt. We
          have a lot to put into place now.

                      JOE FOSTER
            Don't mention it. And Newt, I'm
            sorry about the way things are. I
            wish there was something I could
            do.

                      NEWT
            Leave me on the air, Joe. Just
            leave me on the air.

Newt and Charles leave the room and Joe sits at his desk and
shakes his head.

INT. DEN - NIGHT

VOICES of Newt and Charles doing an old radio bit play from
top of the line speakers.

Newt sits on the floor in front of his stereo listening to
old tapes of his program.

Veronica enters the room and Newt turns the volume down. He
laughs which causes him to cough.

                      NEWT
            We were good.

Veronica shakes her head in agreement

                      VERONICA
            Are you coming to bed?

                      NEWT
            Not yet. I want to go through some
            more tapes first.

                      VERONICA
             You and Charlie were awfully close
            then.

                      NEWT
             Yeah. Too bad he had to ruin
            everything by becoming a suit.

                      VERONICA
             He did that for you, you know. He's
            pulled your butt out of the frying
            pan so many times.

                      NEWT
             Hmmph.

                    VERONICA
          One thing is for certain, dying
          doesn't make you any less stubborn.
          Well, good night.

Before she leaves, Newt grabs her hand and holds it. For the
first time he seems vulnerable.

                    NEWT
          Stay up with me?

Veronica sits down with Newt and they listen to another tape.

FLASHBACK -- INT. RADIO STUDIO - DAY

A younger Newt and Charles perform their radio show together.

                    CHARLES
          You've offended everyone, Newt.
          They all hung up.

                    NEWT
          Serves them right, Charlie baby.
          Got to be strong to call my show.
          Strong and smart. You know, that's
          what this world lacks most. Strong
          and smart people. You can find
          someone who's strong; you can find
          someone who's smart. But not both.
          And you got to have some common
          sense. No one has common sense
          these days, you know.

                    CHARLES
          And why is that, Newt?

                    NEWT
          Glad you asked. Cause I'd love to
          tell you.

                    CHARLES
          I'm sure you would.

                    NEWT
          It's our government

                    CHARLES
          Our government?

                    NEWT
          Well, more precisely, our form of
          government.
                              (MORE)

                              NEWT (CONT'D)
          A democracy is a great concept on
          paper, but the reality is a bit
          different. You know why? Because
          democracy doesn't allow for common
          sense. Sure there are laws for
          practically everything, but you
          can't have a law that covers every
          possible variant of human behavior
          and every circumstance. For
          example, you may have heard this
          story in the news yesterday. In New
          York, this guy this thug, tried to
          mug this little old man. Demanded
          his wallet. Said he had a gun.
          Well, this old man, he was, if I
          remember correctly, in his sixties,
          this man pulls out a gun and shoots
          the would-be mugger dead. Dropped
          him right on the street. Now, as it
          turns out, the mugger—or maybe the
          suits would want me to say
          "alleged" mugger—didn't have a gun
          after all. Didn't have any weapon.
          So, this sixty-some-year-old man is
          now up on murder charges. Can you
          believe that? That's ridiculous,
          folks. Listen up, people. If you
          march into someone's life and
          threaten to steal from them or hurt
          them, I don't care if you plan on
          actually doing it or not. Bam.
          You're dead. And good riddance. As
          far as I'm concerned, it's hunting
          season and you're wearing a nice 12-
          point rack. End of story. (beat)
          Now, speaking of nice racks, let's
          go to Gina at the traffic desk.
          Gina, I hear the 405's a mess.

INT. DEN - NIGHT

The cassette of Newt's radio show ends.

Newt has fallen asleep in Veronica's lap. She is stroking his
hair.

DREAM SEQUENCE

SOFT RHYTHMIC MUSIC. Newt drifts slowly toward a bright white
light ahead of him. A tunnel with a light at the end.

A figure can just barely be made out in the bright light.
Before Newt makes it halfway...

MONTAGE

Clips from ENTERTAINMENT TONIGHT, ACCESS HOLLYWOOD, and
EXTRA, show the hosts of each program discussing Newt's radio
program stunt to stay on the air until he dies.

INT. RADIO STATION, STUDIO - MORNING

The studio and station offices are a buzz with activity.
Assistants, engineers, and others running back and forth
doing various tasks to prepare for the show.

The station owners are present and watching from a listening
room next to Newt's studio.

A RADIO PROMO plays on the speakers as Newt sit down at his
console preparing to go on the air.

Reed and Laura act nervous because of the situation.

A TOUCH-TONE PHONE, FOLLOWED BY FOUR RINGS.

                         STATELY VOICE
             Hello.

                         NEWT
             Yes, is this heaven?

                         STATELY VOICE
             No, this is Iowa.

CLICK.

                         ANNOUNCER
             Touch that dial and lightning will
             strike you down. This is the
             Countdown to Dead-Air with the Newt-
             man on WKAL.

The "On Air" sign LIGHTS.

                         NEWT
             Good morning boys and girls. Well,
             as I'm sure you have guessed by all
             the new promos and all the hype up
             to this point this is day one of
             the Countdown to Dead-Air.
                         (MORE)

                        NEWT (CONT'D)
            That's right we will be counting
            the days, hours and minutes until I
            pass away and cease to exist as you
            know me. So let's get started.
            (beat) I am finding that death is a
            lonely business. You would think
            that people would want to come by
            one last time to say good-bye, but
            no. No, they would rather wait
            until you're dead then say things
            about you. And I don't blame them.
            I mean, what do you say to a living
            corpse on time share? It's got to
            be uncomfortable. I wouldn't know
            what to say and I get paid to talk.
            Do you ask how a dying person how
            he is doing? Do you ask what they
            have planned for tomorrow? No, I
            don't blame my friends for not
            coming by to see me off. It's okay.
            I've got my wife and my radio
            family. I know it's hard on them
            and I truly appreciate what they
            are going through now to allow me
            this last selfish pleasure.

INTERCUT: NEWT'S VO IS HEARD AS WE CUT TO THESE VARIOUS
SCENES

INT. CAR - MORNING

The business man sits in his car again in rush hour traffic.

INT. OFFICE - MORNING

The secretary listens to Newt's show on Internet radio in her
cubicle at work. A co-worker stands next to her to listen as
well.

EXT. CONSTRUCTION SITE - MORNING

The group of construction workers listen to Newt on their
radio while taking a break.

EXT. JOG PATH - MORNING

The male jogger runs and listening to Newt on his headphones.

BACK TO SCENE

                    NEWT

I'd like to begin by reading part of an essay by Robert Bloch, one of entertainment's greatest writers. For those of you that don't recognize his name, he is the author of the original Psycho novel. I'm reading this now because I think Robert summed up some feelings about death better than I ever could, so instead of trying I'll just read what he has to say. Speaking of his own imminent demise, 'Once word gets around—once the cat is let out of the body-bag—people will start calling to inquire how I am. Actually they won't all be all that curious about me; what they'll really want to know is about a visitor called Death. Death will be coming to our house soon for an indefinite stay, but while he's there this unwelcome guest must be treated as a member of the family. And that's what will make callers curious. What's it like, living with Death twenty-four hours a day? Does he make special demands on our attention, interfere with household routine, disturb my comfort, change the ways I eat or sleep? Do we worry about him constantly, keep him first and foremost in our thoughts night and day? Right now I can't give full answers to these questions but expect to be able to do so soon. Very soon. One thing is already clear—we don't look forward to having him around. And we'll be anxious for him to depart. Except that when he leaves he won't go alone. He won't go alone, but he won't take all of me with him, either. A part will still remain behind, until paper crumbles, film dissolves, and memories fade. Who knows? By the time these things happen, you and I, somewhere or someplace, may meet again. Anyway, it's nice to think so. See you later.

                  (MORE)

                    NEWT (CONT'D)
I hope.' (beat) I'll tell ya,
people are afraid of death and
treat it as a bad thing. I think we
need to wash away the taboo of
death and bring it out into the
light. It's funny, well not really,
but the way people are acting and
looking at me, even right now...

Laura looks away from Newt after staring at him.

                    NEWT
You would think I was already dead.
A walking corpse. Now I know I look
bad. You will have to take my word
for it, but there is no need to
stare. People, death is inevitable.
Get over it. Get ready for it. It's
coming I guarantee you—sooner than
later for many of us. Death is like
the ugly by-product of life and we
all try to ignore it exists—and
that's kind of silly. It's gonna
happen to all of us. Let's talk
about, let's discuss our fears and
objections. I know I have a couple.
It's interesting, all my life I
never thought about dying. Death
never crossed my mind, and that
made sense to me. Why spend
precious moments of life dwelling
about non-life? Where is the logic
there? Emily Dickenson wrote
countless poems about death and I
have to wonder, did she really live
if she spent so much time in death?
Did it make her death any easier
for her? I'm telling you life is to
be lived. Who knows what is on the
other side of life. Anyway, my
point is that I never thought about
death until I began to die.
Interesting. Even now I have been
so busy dying that I don't really
have many words of wisdom other
than: live life and what will come
will come. Deep huh? Well, no one
ever gave me any awards for being a
philosopher. I'm just a schmuck
with a voice for radio. So let's
hear it folks. What do you have to
say about death?
                    (MORE)

                    NEWT (CONT'D)
          Now, I don't want to hear any
          stories about how your old granny
          Fanny died or how your dog was run
          over and it was a life-changing
          experience for you. I want to know
          what you think about death. The
          phone lines are open, it's your
          last chance to speak with the Newt-
          Man, so you better make it count.
          We'll take our first caller after
          this break.

Newt pushes back from the console.

Laura enters the studio and gives him a mug of coffee.

                    NEWT
          Has Veronica arrived yet?

                    LAURA
          Not yet. I'll let you know.

Newt gives a thumbs-up to the station managers who smile
cordially. Newt prepares to go back on the air.

Laura exits the studio.

                    NEWT
          This is the Newt-Man. You're on the
          air.

                    BRIAN
              (sarcastically)
          Wow is this really the Newt-Man? I
          never thought I would ever talk to
          you.

                    NEWT
          Who is this, some moronic teenager
          ditching his remedial English
          class, or could it be those two
          homos Mark and Brian?

                    MARK
          For a dying guy, you're still
          quick.

                    NEWT
          Quicker than you could ever hope to
          be.

                    MARK
          Yeah, but the difference between us
          is that you'll be dead soon. We can
          at least speed up.

                    BRIAN
          So, how does it feel to know we
          will finally rule the drive-time
          hours?

                    NEWT
          The only thing you guys will ever
          rule is each other.

                    MARK
          Seriously, it's been nice having
          you as a competitor…

                    BRIAN
          Though we never really thought you
          competed that well. We will miss
          beating you in the ratings each
          week.

                    NEWT
          That probably isn't the only thing
          you've been beating.

                    MARK
          So I guess this means you won't be
          making Dude Night?

                    NEWT
          You know, I wouldn't normally miss
          out on such debauchery, but I do
          have a previous engagement.

                    MARK
          Good to know you've made your peace
          with it.

                    BRIAN
          Speaking of pieces, what's your
          wife going to be doing later?

                    NEWT
             (jokingly)
          I will come back from the dead if
          you even call my wife. Thanks for
          calling, guys. As if I wasn't
          already feeling bad enough you had
          to start my program on a lull. But
          then, I guess you guys are used to
          lulls on your show.

Newt cuts Mark & Brian off before they can respond.

                    NEWT
          Okay, over the course of this show
          I, Newt Richardson, will be
          expounding on some of the things I
          believe you, and I mean all
          humankind, should do before death
          claims you. I have taken the
          liberty to write a few lists of
          things and here now is the first of
          such lists: This one is a list of
          must-see movies. Okay, in no random
          order we have: Casablanca, Lawrence
          of Arabia—on the wide screen
          only—Citizen Kane, the original
          Willy Wonka and the Chocolate
          Factory, Shindlers's List, the Star
          Wars double trilogy, and any movie
          with Kevin Costner. Even
          Waterworld. I mean, so what if it
          cost more money than Rwanda's GNP,
          it was a cool movie. The man had
          gills! Cameron's Avatar was very
          cool--basically Costner's Dances
          with Wolves on an alien planet.
          Also Zombieland was awesome. Just
          the opening credits were beyond
          cool and then you give us Bill
          Murray. Freakin' A awesome! That's
          a short list, maybe I'll think of
          some more later. While I am at it,
          let's get another list out of the
          way. Things you must do before you
          die. In no particular order: make
          love in a move theater, plant a
          garden, learn to play an
          instrument, fall in love at least
          once, respect your parents—unless
          of course they beat you, then you
          have my permission to take an ax to
          them while they sleep—get a full
          body massage, buy a homeless person
          dinner and read the Bible all the
          way through. Well, look at that my
          phone lines are all aglow. Okay,
          caller you're on the air. What do
          you have to say for yourself?

The first caller sounds like a male in his early twenties.
The caller sounds like someone who wants to sound cool on the
radio but instead sounds like a complete imbecile.

                    CALLER 1
          Uh hello?

                    NEWT
          Yes, caller you're on the air.

                    CALLER 1
          Hello Newt?

                    NEWT
          Yes. Speak, I command thee!

                    CALLER 1
          Oh. Hey man, I just wanted to
          say...you know...good riddance and
          all.

                    NEWT
          Well, thank you caller. And your
          name is…?

                    CALLER 1
          Uh, John. And I just wanted to say
          to you man that I think your death
          is long overdue. I wish your death
          could have come sooner. Then I
          wouldn't have had to listen to your
          stupid show for so long, you know
          man?

                    NEWT
          No, actually I don't Johnny. You
          see I possess the intelligence to
          turn something off I don't like.
          Like right now, for instance.

Newt disconnects the caller.

                    NEWT
          I want to thank Johnny for being a
          prime example of the stupidity that
          runs rampant in our streets each
          day. God bless you, Johnny. But
          Johnny reminds me of something I
          have to say about human beings
          before I depart this world. I
          believe that people are
          fundamentally stupid and evil. Take
          a look around you. There is
          stupidity everywhere. Take my
          station managers. They have got to
          be the stupidest and most evil
          people of all.
                         (MORE)

                    NEWT (CONT'D)
          They wouldn't know good taste if it
          leapt up and bit them in the ass. I
          think stupidity should be illegal.
          Lock the people in jail and throw
          away the key.

INTERCUT: NEWT'S VO IS HEARD AS WE CUT TO THESE VARIOUS
SCENES

EXT. CONSTRUCTION SITE - DAY

The Construction workers are laughing and pointing at each
other during this bit.

INT. OFFICE - DAY

The Secretary is laughing and a co-worker walks by and stops
to listen as well.

BACK TO SCENE

                    NEWT (CONT'D)
          By all means, we need to keep these
          people from propagating. The tough
          thing about a Stupidity Law is how
          to enforce it. Who decides who is
          being stupid. I mean, we all do
          stupid things now and then. So the
          people we need to go after are the
          ones that do stupid things all the
          time. The people who are just
          downright idiotic, moronic and
          irrecoverably dumb. These people
          must be stopped I say! You know the
          type: twelve items in the ten items
          or less line at the grocery store;
          won't move to the right when faster
          traffic comes up behind them on a
          freeway; leaves their turn signal
          on for twenty miles. I'm here to
          tell you if there were a Stupidity
          Law, the world would be a much
          safer and better place. Of course,
          the very politicians who would
          create such a law would then all
          have to surrender themselves over
          to the law since being a politician
          would be a capital offensive under
          the Stupidity Law.
                    (MORE)

                    NEWT (CONT'D)
Well, okay, now that I have that
out of my system let's take another
caller. Hello caller, you're on the
air.

                    CALLER 2
Yeah. Hi Newt. You forgot one thing
on your list of things to do before
you die.

                    NEWT
And what is that?

                    CALLER 2
Have a child. There's nothing more
beautiful or exciting as having a
kid.

                    NEWT
And nothing as ugly as a red,
bloody, wrinkly newborn screaming
24 hours a day and throwing up on
your neck. Let me tell you
something people. Kids, they were
never for me. In fact, I could
never understand why anyone would
want one. What kind of investment
is a child? If I told you about a
company you could invest $1 million
into over 18 years and the only
return on the investment was, ah,
pride or whatever, would you write
that check? I don't think so.
Children are totally dependent, and
they're completely stupid. You sit
there in front of them saying crap
like oogi, googi, floogi. How
stupid is that? Grown-ups waste
hours every day just entertaining a
child. Kids turn adults into
children. I had a friend, I won't
say his na...What the hell? I'll
tell you his name; I'm a dying man.
Frank Rubel was his name. The great
radio personality, Frank Rubel.
Have you heard of him? No, you
haven't. Why? Because he had a kid.
That's right. Let me be the first
to say that Frank could have been a
great talk show host. I met him 20
or so years ago when we were both
starting out. On the radio, that
man was smooth.
                    (MORE)

                    NEWT (CONT'D)
He could tell a story, and no one
had the wit that Frank had—yours
truly excluded, of course. I always
thought that Frank had a great
career ahead of him, but he never
made it. That's because he had a
kid. Before you knew it, he refused
to work evenings because he had to
pick up the kid. The kid sapped
every creative energy from him. It
didn't take long for him to become
completely boring. Not a good trait
for a radio man. Having a kid was
Frank's downfall. It was like his
kid was more important than his
job. What a shmuck. (beat) Caller
are you still there?

                    CALLER 2
Yeah. So what you're saying is that
Frank was wrong to put his family
ahead of his career.

                    NEWT
No, I never said that.

                    CALLER 2
Sure you did. You said it was like
Frank's kid was more important than
his job.

                    NEWT
Yeah, but I was exactly saying…

                    CALLER 2
You know, people like you don't
deserve the privilege of being a
parent.

The Caller hangs up.

Newt sits somewhat stunned.

FLASHBACK, INT. APARTMENT - DAY

Newt and Veronica, in their 20s, sit in a small apartment
high above the city. The apartment is moderately furnished
and not flashy.

Newt and Veronica are shouting.

                    NEWT
You know how I feel about children.

                    VERONICA
No, I don't. We don't talk about
it.

                    NEWT
I told you I want to focus on my
job first. Why can't you support me
on this? You know how much radio
means to me and I won't be able to
really succeed if I have to stay up
all night every night waiting on a
screaming baby. It's not the right
time, Veronica.

                    VERONICA
When is the right time, Newt? This
is serious for me. I'm not getting
younger. We need to start
considering if and when we are
going to have children.

                    NEWT
Okay, let's talk about serious.
Here's what's serious: We pay $300
per month for this dump, which we
can't afford. Our car hasn't had
its oil changed in 15,000 miles,
because we can't afford it. Yet, I
come home yesterday and find a new
toaster. Did we need a toaster? No.
You burn toast one day because
you're too lazy to watch it and
it's the toaster's fault. Get rid
of the old. That's your solution.
Now let's talk about making more
money. Do you have a job yet? How
many resumes did you send out
today? Don't answer. Let me guess.
A big fat zero. Oh, but I'm sure
the phone was ringing off the hook.
How many interviews did you set up
today? Don't answer. Let me guess.
A big fat zero. Way to go, honey.
So until you're willing to bring
home a paycheck, we can't afford a
kid. Not on my salary right now.

                    VERONICA
You know we have a savings account.

                              NEWT
                    Great idea. Let's spend that. Let's
                    throw our future to the wind and
                    waste that money on a child. Forget
                    the Mercedes. Let's just throw that
                    money away on diapers to catch our
                    child's piss.

                              VERONICA
                    You can be so cold and heartless
                    sometimes? A child isn't a
                    nuisance. It isn't an investment.
                    It is a privilege. And, quite
                    frankly, you don't deserve the
                    privilege of being a parent.

This sentence echoes several times as we go back to present
time.

BACK TO SCENE

Newt sit quietly at the console.

Reed stares at Newt waiting for him to being talking again.
He knocks lightly on the glass to get Newt's attention. When
that doesn't work he wraps harder until he is darn near
breaking the glass.

Finally Newt awakes from his daydream.

                              NEWT
                    We had better take a break.

INT. RADIO STATION, STUDIO - AFTERNOON

The office is bustling. Charles stands near a desk, holding a
phone. He covers the mouth piece.

                              CHARLES
                    Where's that fax?

An assistant hands a piece of paper to Charles. He reads it.

                              CHARLES
                    I got it, Joe. That company has
                    never had any guts anyway. Let them
                    walk.

Charles spots Veronica entering the front door.

Veronica enters the station and sees Charles. She waves to
him. He gives a hand signal to hold-on.

                    CHARLES
          Okay, I'll tell him. Yeah.

Charles hangs up and approaches Veronica.

                    VERONICA
          Hello Charles. It's been a while,
          how are you doing?

                    CHARLES
          I'm fine. I'm surprised to see you
          here.

                    VERONICA
          So am I. Don't let him know I'm
          here though. I want to watch for a
          while. Okay?

                    CHARLES
          Sure (beat) I'm sorry.

                    VERONICA
          Thank you. How is he doing?

                    CHARLES
          Well, we just lost our third
          advertiser, syndication says the
          affiliates are jittery, and Newt
          just pissed off a nun.

They start walking toward the studio.

                    VERONICA
          Wow. Normal day.

                    CHARLES
          Yeah, same old Newt. I think he's
          getting a bit tired.

                    VERONICA
          Yeah, I could hear it in his voice
          on the way over.

They see Newt talking in the studio.

                    VERONICA
          Ugh and he looks awful.

                    CHARLES
          He has been going since six this
          morning without a break. That's
          nine hours. If you want, you can
          listen in my office. I'll make sure
          he doesn't know you're here.

                         VERONICA
               I will. Thanks.

The two are interrupted by an ASSISTANT who hands some papers
to Charles.

                         CHARLES
               Will you excuse me?

                         VERONICA
               Of course.

Charles walks away.

Veronica leans up against the studio window and watches Newt.
He has his back to her so he cannot see she is there.

INT. RADIO STATION - NIGHT

It is near the end of the first day.

Newt is still going strong, though noticeably tired. He
coughs on occasion.

                         NEWT
               The clinical explanation of death
               is that your heart stops. Your
               brain, not knowing that your heart
               has stopped, is technically alive
               for another three to four minutes.
               For many, I'm thinking anyone in
               the Kennedy family, the exact
               opposite is true. Your digestive
               track is the last to be told that
               you're dead and continues to digest
               for the next twenty-four hours.
               Isn't that amazing.

INTERCUT: NEWT'S VO IS HEARD AS WE CUT TO THESE VARIOUS
SCENES

INT. HOME - NIGHT

The Business Man from the car is now at home. Dressed
casually he sits at a dinner table eating. He listens to Newt
on a stereo system.

INT. CONSTRUCTION TRAILER - NIGHT

The Construction Workers are in a trailer at the construction
site listening to Newt while drinking beer.

INT. OFFICE - NIGHT

The Secretary is still at work listening to Newt on her
Internet radio.

BACK TO SCENE

                    NEWT (CONT'D)
        I'll tell you what, I plan on
        having one heck of a great last
        meal because I want my body to
        enjoy it well after I'm dead. It's
        the least I can do considering what
        I've put my body through all these
        years. Also, blood remains viable
        for several hours then begins to
        settle downward in mortis,
        something my old high school
        girlfriend used to suffer from,
        takes place two to six hours after
        death depending on circumstances,
        then reverses two to three days
        later. Okay, here's where the
        squeamish might want to turn down
        the volume. The flesh decomposes,
        then the veins and skin turn nice
        shades of blue, purple, green and
        black. Certainly something to
        remember as you attempt to color
        code the attire you wish to be
        buried in. Next, the softer tissues
        turn to jelly and the cornea of the
        eye becomes cloudy—that is, before
        the eye begins to melt into their
        sockets altogether. Finally, the
        skin pulls away from the lips,
        leaving a small grin. This makes me
        wonder if dying is really that bad
        of a thing. Heck if my corpse can
        grin after the fact, then death
        can't be all that bad. But, I'll
        tell ya, after reading that, I want
        to be cremated. I want to go out in
        a huge ball of fire. God bless
        those shuttle astronauts, you
        remember? Blew themselves all to
        dust in a fraction of a second.
                (MORE)

> NEWT (CONT'D)
>
> Now that's the way to go. Or like
> my friend Hunter S. Thompson. His
> friends shot his ass out of a huge
> fist shaped canon. Those are true
> friends. Unfortunately, the only
> ball of fire this old decrepit body
> is going to see in the next twenty-
> four hours will have to come out my
> butt as a blue flame. But hey, as
> frail as I am, that just might blow
> me to dust. And isn't that what
> they say, "ashes to ashes and dust
> to dust." Hey, what's the Bible say
> about that? Anyone? Something about
> man came from the dust and to the
> dust he shall return. So be it! I
> proclaim right now, I, Newt
> Richardson, of sound mind and
> deteriorating body, do so wish for
> my remains to be put in a boat, set
> on fire and cast out into the
> ocean. Just like some Viking
> warrior. That would be so cool. Can
> we arrange something like that? Set
> me on fire and push me out to see.
> Oh wait, that reminds me of a song.
> Let's see if we can find that. Yes?
> Okay, a little musical interlude
> while I go to freshen up. Don't go
> away. Barry Manilow's "Lay Me Down
> and Roll Me Out to Sea" fades in as
> the song is broadcast out over the
> air. Newt nearly falls as he tries
> to stand from his chair. Everyone
> goes to help him and he steadies
> himself and assures everyone he is
> fine.
>> (to Reed)
> Let's play some old clips for the
> next couple of breaks, all right? I
> want to rest.

> REED
> Sure Newt, I've got some carts
> ready to do.

INT. GREEN ROOM - NIGHT

A small couch, table and a refrigerator along with a long
table topped with sandwiches, snacks, soft drinks, coffee and
medical supplies.

Newts enters along with Charles.

                CHARLES
        Sit down.

He helps Newt to the couch then checks out the table.

                CHARLES
        Coffee?

                NEWT
        Water.

Charles gets a water and picks up a paper plate.

                CHARLES
        Sounds like the show is going well.
        Tuna salad?

                NEWT
        No. (beat) The show is great. I
        think we're really turning some
        heads—not the least of which is
        Foster's.

                CHARLES
        No doubt. Chips?

                NEWT
        No thanks.

Charles hands him his water.

                NEWT
        That's okay, though. The listeners
        are loving it. I've had some great
        calls.

                CHARLES
        Yeah. Good stuff. Although you look
        and sound tired.

                NEWT
        Yeah, well I feel tired.

Charles picks up a syringe.

                CHARLES
        Shot of adrenaline?

                NEWT
        Nah. For our guests.

Charles smiles. Newt smiles back. Charles brings the plate
over and sits besides Newt.

                    CHARLES
          Seriously. Are you okay? You don't
          look so good.

                    NEWT
          I'm tired. Really tired. But
          overall, I'm okay.

                    CHARLES
          Pain?

                    NEWT
          Some.

                    CHARLES
          Newt, you've made a good run.
          You've made your point. Maybe it's
          time to call it a success and go
          home. You'll be much more
          comfortable there.

                    NEWT
          I can't. I've made this commitment
          and I must see it through.

                    CHARLES
          Look at you. You're a mess. Dead
          tired. In pain.

                    NEWT
          That's what these are for.

Newt holds up a prescription pill vial.

                    NEWT (CONT'D)
          Not a lot of pain. I'm mostly just
          tired. I'm okay, really.

                    CHARLES
          Are you sure?

                    NEWT
          Honest. I can finish this. I want
          to finish this. I need to finish
          this.

                    CHARLES
          Okay, okay.

                    NEWT
          Maybe I will take that coffee,
          though. Extra caffeine.

>
>   CHARLES
>   No problem

Newt lays back on the couch and begins to doze

DREAM SEQUENCE

Again SOFT RHYTHMIC MUSIC. Drifting slowly behind Newt as he drifts toward a bright white light ahead of him. Newts travels a little farther down the tunnel.

BACK TO SCENE

Veronica wakes Newt.

He rolls over.

>   NEWT
>   What are you doing here?

>   VERONICA
>   I couldn't stay away. I love you
>   Newt.

The two hug and kiss.

Charles enters the room in a very somber mood.

>   CHARLES
>   It's not good news, Newt. Many of
>   the syndicates have dropped the
>   show for the nights. They say it's
>   too morbid.

>   NEWT
>   Those spineless jellyfish!

>   VERONICA
>   At least you have this station.

Newt and Veronica turn to Charles who looks down to his feet.

>   NEWT
>   Charles, don't tell me you couldn't
>   keep me on at least one station

>   CHARLES
>   They haven't pulled the plug yet,
>   but Foster is threatening. The
>   show's not working Newt. A lot of
>   people think this is some sort of
>   sick joke.

                        NEWT
            It is Chuck. I'm dying! What more
            of a bad punch line could you think
            of? (calming) So what do they want
            me to do? Did they give you any
            ideas of what they want me to
            change? Or, do they just want me to
            stop?

                        CHARLES
            I promised you I would keep you on
            the air and I meant it. Just lay
            off your pot-shots of the
            management. Give me some time and
            I'll make things right.

                        NEWT
            I hope so. This is my last hurrah
            and I can't risk having it screwed
            up.

Newt leaves the room and Veronica watches after him then
turns to Charles.

                        VERONICA
            I know you will do everything you
            can. Newt does to. He just has a
            hard time expressing it.

INT. RADIO STATION, STUDIO - EARLY MORNING

Newt comes back into the studio and sits down in front of his
microphone.

Veronica and Charles can be seen in the background looking
through the studio glass.

                        NEWT
            It's day two of our little
            countdown and I feel like I can
            make it for another month, at
            least. I'd like to take a moment to
            tell you about an old friend of
            mine. I haven't seen this friend in
            a lot of years, and the fact is I
            don't even know if he is still
            alive. He was a producer of mine
            when I first started this
            illustrious career, and I'm here to
            tell you this man had balls of
            brass. When things were tough he
            was right there biting back twice
            as hard.
                        (MORE)

                    NEWT (CONT'D)
          He wouldn't back down from the
          stuffed shirts for all the money in
          the world. This guy had chutzpah.
          Once, the show he was producing was
          going to do a political skit about
          the president of the time. Well,
          the stuffed shirts wanted to ax the
          piece because they were afraid it
          was too controversial. I mean come
          on, claiming the president is a
          closet transvestite who has sex
          with sheep in the rose garden
          seemed appropriate at the time.
          Well, this guy wouldn't back down.
          He stuck with his show and told the
          stuffed shirts if they didn't have
          the guts to air the skit he would
          take the show to another station.
          Low and behold, the stuffed shirts
          backed down. Of course, he was
          bluffing. There wasn't another
          radio station in the fifty states
          that would touch the program at
          that time, but he bluffed and kept
          the show's integrity. This producer
          was a good man. No, a great man! He
          had come from the gene pool of
          champions.

Newt looks at Charles and continues with his monologue.

                    NEWT (CONT'D)
          In fact, I heard a rumor that this
          guy was actually spawned from the
          loins of Seattle Slew and breast
          feed by Mother Teresa. And I
          believe it. This was a man of true
          integrity and honor. I miss my
          friend. I hope he can hear this
          now, 'cause I won't be able to say
          it again. Wherever you are, I love
          and respect you. You gave me the
          chance to do what I wanted to do
          and I thank you from my heart.

Veronica puts a hand on Charles shoulder.

Newt turns away from the window and leads into a rousing sing-
a-long of a song parodying death based on the music Wizard of
Oz's "We're Off to See the Wizard." The new chorus is "We're
Off to See the Reaper."

INT. STUDIO - LATER

Newt is pale, tired and weak. He coughs more frequently.

MUSIC from the program's bumper lead-in ends.

Sitting with Newt are four men, PASTOR RANDY HILL (a 40-ish charismatic young man), RABBI HARVEY STEINBERG (bearded man in his sixties who looks young for his age), JASON PATRICK (young, wide eyed, child-like), and BOB ROGERS (bald, middle aged, well dressed).

Each wears headphones and sit in front of microphones.

> NEWT (CONT'D)
> Ladies and gentlemen, I am pleased
> to have joining me in the studio
> representatives of some major
> religions of the world. On my right
> is Pastor Randy Hill, pastor of
> Glory and Grace Church in Palmdale.
> Next to him is Rabbi Harvey
> Steinberg of the East End
> Congregation in West Hollywood, a
> favorite spot for our Jewish
> celebrity friends. Next is Jason
> Patrick, head of the Southern
> California Chapter of the Church of
> Newism, which although not a major
> religion, I'm told it's gaining
> followers at a high rate. Finally,
> on my left is Bob Rogers, organizer
> of The Buddhist Society of Los
> Angeles, a membership organization
> numbering more than 200. (beat) let
> me start with you, Mr. Rogers.
> Yours is not a particularly
> Buddhist-sounding name.

> BOB
> You don't have to have a name like
> Siddhartha Gautama, our founder, to
> be Buddhist.

> NEWT
> Just bald?

> BOB
> No, Newt. That's a stereotype. I
> was bald before I was Buddhist. We
> have many hairy followers.

NEWT
Just how prevalent is Buddhism
around the world?

BOB
Actually, Newt, about 6 percent of
the world's population is
Buddhist—that's more than 300
million people. There are not all
that many Buddhists in the United
States. However, the number is
growing. The overwhelming majority
are in Asia, Indochina and Tibet.

NEWT
Right, Tibet. Richard Gere was just
elected mayor there, I believe. (to
technician's booth) Could someone
check that for me.

BOB
I don't think they have a mayor,
Newt.

NEWT
Just monks and mountains, I
suppose. Anyway, Bob, give us a
short summary of what Buddhists
believe.

BOB
Well, Newt, they believe many
different things. The religion was
founded as a form of Hinduism.
Buddhists, first, believe in
Buddha—or the enlightened being.

NEWT
Now, who is Buddha?

BOB
Buddha is not a who. Buddha is not
a god or the creator of the
universe. Buddha is simply a state
of enlightenment. Anybody can be a
Buddha.

NEWT (SINGING)
I'm a Buddha, you're a Buddha,
wouldn't you like to be a Buddha
too.

                    BOB
They also believe in karma and in
meditation. And they believe that
suffering is caused by material
things.

                    NEWT
I know what you mean. I suffered
for a week after someone rear-ended
my Mercedes.

                    BOB
Actually, Newt, the desire itself
for material things is what causes
your suffering.

                    NEWT
All right then. And I thought it
was the cancer. (beat) Moving on.
Pastor Hill, why is it non-
denominational pastors don't wear
funny costumes like the other
faiths?

                    PASTOR HILLRABBI
Well, we don't dress funny as you
say, no disrespect to these other
faiths, we just talk funny when the
spirit moves.

                    NEWT
Fair enough. Most people are
familiar with the Christian way of
life. That there is one God. That
Jesus was born as the Son of God to
save our souls, that there is a
heaven and hell—and purgatory,
which, if I understand it
correctly, is simply a place to
have a drink while they prepare
your table in the nonsmoking or
smoking section.

                    PASTOR HILL
The difference is that you don't
get your choice of sections, Newt.

                    NEWT
Right. Well, give us all
understanding about the scope of
Christianity.

                    PASTOR HILL
Well, Newt, first let me correct
you. Purgatory is a predominantly
Catholic belief. Christianity as a
whole is the most prevalent
religion in the world, representing
a third of the world. The basic
tenet, as you said, is a belief in
Jesus Christ, the Son of God, who
came to Earth to die for our sins.
Christians also believe the Bible
is the Word of God. The Catholic,
Protestant, Eastern Orthodox,
Anglican and a host of other
churches all practice a form of
Christianity.

                    NEWT
Okay. Next up is Rabbi Steinberg,
same question. Please give us a
general understanding of Judaism.

                    RABBI STEINBERG
Well, Judaism is the oldest
religion, founded in the Middle
East. It is widely known that Jews
were persecuted by the Germans in
World War II. However, most don't
realize that Jews were also
persecuted by the Romans, thus
resulting in what is known as the
Jewish Diaspora—meaning that the
Jews dispersed from the Middle East
and settled in various parts of the
world.

                    NEWT
And how many Jews are out there?

                    RABBI STEINBERG
There are about 15 million Jews
living in such diverse places as
Israel, North America and Russia.

                    NEWT
And the basic tenets of the
religion?

                    RABBI STEINBERG
Judaism is actually similar to
Christianity in some ways. We
believe in one God. We also have
heaven and hell.
                    (MORE)

49.

                    RABBI STEINBERG (CONT'D)
          However, we believe in the Torah,
          not the Bible. We also believe in a
          Messiah, but we don't believe that
          it is Jesus. Nor do we believe that
          God has sent the Messiah to Earth
          yet.

                    NEWT
          Isn't the Torah the five books of
          Moses from the Old Testament?

                    RABBI STEINBERG
          It is. But it also includes some
          other scriptures and literature.

                    NEWT
          Thank you, Rabbi. (beat) Turning
          our attention to Mr. Patrick. I
          don't believe I've ever heard of
          the Church of Newism. Newtism, yes.
          I practice that constantly, but
          usually by myself.

                    JASON
          Well, Newt, the Church of Newism
          has been around for some 90 years.

                    NEWT
          Really?

                    JASON
          Yes. It was created by Dr. Howard
          Burnhard in San Francisco in 1906,
          right after the big San Francisco
          earthquake.

                    NEWT
          Ah-huh.

                    JASON
          In fact, as the story foes, after
          watching his beloved San Francisco
          fall to the ground, the ever-
          optimistic Mr. Burnhard coined the
          phrase "out with the old, in with
          the new." That's the basic tenet of
          Newsim.

                    NEWT
          So anything aged must go.

                    JASON
          Not exactly, Newt. Newsim allows
          for the old.
                              (MORE)

                    JASON (CONT'D)
We just believe that God reaches
out to his people through
everything new.

                    NEWT
Hmmm.

                    JASON
It makes perfect sense, if you
think about it. We desire newness.
We buy new cars, new houses, new
furniture. New makes us happy. New
fulfills a need. New comforts our
soul.

                    NEWT
I'm with you, Jason. But then, how
do you explain a New Coke?

                    JASON
Well, ah, the Lord works in
mysterious ways.

                    NEWT
He does indeed. (beat) Well before
things get any more mysterious,
let's take a time-out for this word
from L.A. Brewing Company, where
their motto is "you're going to die
anyway, so drink up."

                    REED
Clear.

Newt addresses the group.

                    NEWT
All right gentlemen, this is where
it should get fun. I want to
discuss where you each believe we
go once we die. Specifically me.
Let's try to spunk it up a bit, but
remember no cursing—this is radio.
And no biting.

                    BOB
Newt, as a Buddhist I am a
pacifist. I cannot get into
arguments or physical violence.

                    NEWT
That's fine, Bob. You sit there and
"ooomm," while the rest of us have
some fun.

PASTOR HILL
Well, Newt, scripture does tell us,
"When words are many, sin is not
absent, but he who hold his tongue
is wise." Proverbs 10:19. We should
not willingly participate in
arguments or folly.

RABBI STEINBERG
I agree.

NEWT
Guys. Guys. Don't let me down here.
I have a show to do and it needs to
be exciting.

REED
Ten seconds, Newt.

NEWT
Let's have some fun, and if you
feel like punching someone, go with
your feeling. Okay?

REED
You're live.

The MUSIC cues coming out of commercial.

NEWT
Welcome back. If you've just tuned
in, we're speaking with several
experts about religion and the
afterlife. (beat) I want to now
turn our discussion to the subject
at hand—death. Specifically, my
death. (beat) Now, I know you are
all probably very reluctant to
guess what my afterlife will...

PASTOR HILL
You're going to hell.

NEWT
Well, maybe not so reluctant, after
all. So, you feel I should dress
cool.

PASTOR HILL
I'm kidding, Newt. But you are a
sinner, like all of us. So, to get
into heaven, you must be repentive
for your sins and ask Christ for
forgiveness.
(MORE)

                    PASTOR HILL (CONT'D)
          Whether you are remorseful or not,
          that's not for me to judge. Only
          God knows what is in your heart.
          Although, for me, your earlier
          comments cast some doubt.

                    NEWT
          Okay.

                    JASON
          You've had a long career—out with
          the old.

                    NEWT
          What, you looking for a job, Jason?
          I already know I'm dying. I'm
          searching for advice on afterlife.

                    BOB
          Well, Buddhists believe that one is
          in a constant state of
          reincarnation until he or she has
          reached Nirvana—that is, until a
          person reaches a state of perfect
          blessedness form the extinction of
          individual existence and the
          absorption of the soul by the
          supreme spirit, or by the
          elimination of all individual
          desires.

                    NEWT
          Come again?

                    BOB
          You'll be back.

                    JASON
          We believe that, after death,
          everyone comes back again.

                    NEWT
          Reincarnation? If I believed in
          reincarnation, I would want to come
          back as a Kobe Beef cow. They live
          the life. First they are suspended
          in air, so they don't touch the
          ground, they are fed organic wheat
          and barley, and drink sake and beer
          all day, and then little Japanese
          masseuses come in and rub them down
          so they stay tender.
                    (MORE)

                    NEWT (CONT'D)
Basically they hang around, get
stoned on beer and sake and get rub
downs. What's not to love about
that?

                    JASON
Well, Newt, our concept is similar
to reincarnation, but we come back
as something new. Not necessarily a
new person. If you were a person in
one life, you wouldn't be a person
in your next life. That's now new.

                    NEWT
So you'd come back as a new, say,
baseball mitt or Alfa Romeo or
restaurant.

                    JASON
Kind of. It has to be something new
to life as we know it. You'll
probably come back as a new 3D
movie.
        (To others)
They're big now.

                    NEWT
You're big too, Bob. A big ass...

                    PASTOR HILL
Watch it. You've come so far.

                    NEWT
...assembly line of information.
(beat) Rabbi, comments?

                    RABBI STEINBERG
Good luck.

                    NEWT
Anything more specific?

                    RABBI STEINBERG
God bless.

                    NEWT
Thanks, Rabbi. They surely have a
position at Hallmark for you.
(beat) Maybe we should try the
phones. Caller what would you like
to add?

                    CALLER 3
You have only a few days to live,
and you're spending 20 minutes of
it talking religion. What a waste
of time.

                    NEWT
A waste of time, huh?

                    CALLER 3
Yeah. Come on, there's no God. When
you're dead, you're gone. That's
the end. It's over. Enter the
worms. You rot in a box.

                    NEWT
So you're an atheist.

                    CALLER 3
I guess so. I don't believe in any
god.

                    NEWT
Well, caller, I respect that
opinion. I think your wrong, but
I'll allow you your opinion. In
fact, a year ago I might have
agreed with you. I'll be honest,
every day for the past year I've
thought about dying. It hasn't just
been on my mind—I've pined over my
unanswered questions and my vague
beliefs. Is there a God? Is there
an afterlife? Does one have a soul?
I don't know. But after a year of
thinking about it, I have reached
one conclusion: I sure hope so.
Even when you're healthy, the
thought of dying is scary. But
here's my life: Every time I wake
up I think, Is this my last day?
Every time I shave I think, Is this
my last razor cut? Is this my last
pizza? Is this my last iced tea? My
last haircut? My last paycheck?
Last water bill? Last red light?
Last hug? Kiss? Heck, my last
caller? So caller I challenge you,
and all doubters out there, live
every day like it could be your
last and see if you suddenly start
considering the prospect of an
afterlife.

                    PASTOR HILL
          That's very good, Newt. There may
          be hope for you yet as long as you
          know Christ.

                    BOB
          Newt, you need to channel your
          energy in meditation to achieve
          what you seek.

          PASTOR HILL   RABBI STEINBERG
What a crock.   What a crock.

                    NEWT
          Ooooo. Tag team. I like this.

Hill and Steinberg smile at each other and give a weak high-
five.

                    JASON
          What about me?

                    ALL
          Shut up!

                    NEWT
          Yeah, that would be new. Let's take
          another caller. Hello, you're on
          the air.

                    CALLER 4
          Well, Newt. I just want to say that
          if God has a sense of humor, you're
          going to heaven.

                    NEWT
          And if he doesn't?

                    CALLER 4
          Don't bend over to stoke the fire.

Newt laughs.

                    NEWT
          Thanks caller. (beat) That brings
          up an interesting point. Both
          Judaism and Christianity have a
          hell. What exactly is hell? Is it a
          place? A state of being? Is it
          fiery hot, like it's shown in the
          movies? Maybe this is hell. Earth
          could be hell. Maybe hell is
          listening to Lady Gaga. Or being
          stuck on the 405.
                    (MORE)

                    NEWT (CONT'D)
Or at FAQ Shwartz in Manhattan on
Christmas Eve. Anyone?

                    PASTOR HILL
Well, the concept of hell comes
from Greek mythology. Hades was
this underworld where the souls of
the unrighteous resided. Hell is
the permanent separation from God.
Is it a place? The scripture seems
to lead us to believe that. But it
is a place as much of mental
discomfort, not so much a place
where one is punished with fire-
tipped spears. You will know you
have wronged and you will regret it
for all eternity.

                    NEWT
That long huh? Kind of like sitting
through The Pursuit of Happyness
with Will Smith. Spending ten bucks
on that was a regret.

                    PASTOR HILL
This is a little more serious.

                    NEWT
Sure. Sure.

                    RABBI STEINBERG
It's important for your
listeners—and you, Newt—to focus on
how to get into heaven, not on
hell? We can control only how we
live every day. If we devote our
daily lives to God, we will follow
the path to heaven. And there will
be no need to define hell.

                    NEWT
That's an interesting point, Rabbi.

                    JASON
Hell is passé. Been there, done
that.

                    NEWT
Appreciate the input Jason. (beat)
So, bottom line guys. Where will I
be going?

                    PASTOR HILL
          If you have prayed the sinner's
          prayer, you will go to heaven. Only
          you and God know if you have truly
          accepted Christ into your life and
          repented for your sins.

                    BOB
          Plan on returning, Newt. I think
          you have a lot left to learn.

                    RABBI STEINBERG
          There is no returning. Your soul
          will move on based on your life and
          how you kept God's law.

                    JASON
          You...

                    NEWT
          Save it.
               (beat)
          Well, unfortunately, we're out of
          time. Let me say this: Life is a
          journey. So is faith. I hope that
          these experts were able to shed
          some light today, maybe even
          provide some answers. But in any
          journey, one never knows what's
          around the next bend.
          Unfortunately, my road is at a dead-
          end. Literally. I thank you all for
          riding with me today.
               (beat)
          I'll be back after this message
          from Sax Roast Beef, where, despite
          what Jason says, you will not find
          dead people ground into their new
          roast beef sandwiches

A RADIO PROMO plays.

The guests take their headphones off and shake Newt's hand as
they leave the studio.

THE SOUND OF A TOUCH-TONE PHONE, FOLLOWED BY FOUR RINGS.

                    STATELY VOICE
          Hello.

                    NEWT
          Yes, is this heaven?

                    STATELY VOICE
          No, this is Iowa.

CLICK.

                    ANNOUNCER
          Touch that dial and lightning will
          strike you down. The Newt-Man on
          WKAL.

INT. RADIO STATION - NIGHT

Newt steps out into the hallway where Pastor Hill and the
others stand chatting (MOS).

Veronica steps into the hall from the Green Room and meets
Newt. They hug affectionately.

                    VERONICA
          That went well.

                    NEWT
          Yeah. No lightning strikes, so I
          guess I didn't piss God off too
          much.

                    VERONICA
          No, but you are always so close.

Pastor Hill steps over to Newt and Veronica and extends his
hand to Newt.

                    PASTOR HILL
          Newt, I wish you well. I wish we
          had more time to talk. I did enjoy
          your show, even it if was a bit
          risqué.

                    NEWT
          Oh, this was nothing tonight.

                    PASTOR HILL
          I know, and that scares me a
          little.

                    VERONICA
          Thank you for coming.

                    PASTOR HILL
          It was my pleasure. (beat) Would
          you mind if I speak with you both,
          a minute?

                    NEWT
          Well, I will need to get back soon.

Newt turns to look at Veronica, who gives him a look like,
come on Newt take some time.

                    NEWT (CONT'D)
          Sure, what the hay. They have some
          old clips they can play. Let's step
          into the Green Room.

INT. GREEN ROOM

Newt steps into the Green room. Veronica and Pastor Hill
follow.

                    PASTOR HILL
          I'll take a Diet Coke if you have
          one.

                    VERONICA
          I'll get it. Newt sit down.

Newt sits on the couch and Pastor Hill sits across from him.

                    NEWT
          So, pastor, what's on your mind?

                    PASTOR HILL
          Well, Newt, I wouldn't be doing my
          job if I didn't stop and ask you if
          you believe in Christ. It is
          important that you have a peace
          about what will happen to you after
          you die. Your wife, as well, should
          have a peace about your afterlife.

                    NEWT
          I appreciate your consideration.

                    PASTOR HILL
          Now, I know you live a worldly
          life. But it is never too late to
          receive the gift of grace from God.

                    NEWT
          Would this be called a death-bed
          conversion?

                    VERONICA
          Newt, this is serious. Can you
          please stop joking for one minute.

Newt realizes how serious Veronica is taking this and settles down to genuinely listen to Pastor Hill.

> PASTOR HILL
> Newt, I think what you are doing
> with your program is very good, and
> courageous. You are taking this
> time to be introspective and search
> your faith. You just choose to do
> it with half the country. But, more
> importantly, you need to repent for
> your sins and ask for forgiveness
> from God and those you have sinned
> against while you were alive.

> NEWT
> I don't think I have that much time
> left.
>   (to Veronica)
> Sorry, a little slip. Won't happen
> again. I promise.

> PASTOR HILL
> I'm serious, Newt. A repentive
> heart is pleasing to God. Please
> think about it.

> NEWT
> Are you open twenty-four hours a
> day?

Veronica gives Newt a dirty look.

> NEWT
> Sorry.

> PASTOR HILL
> Yes I am. Take care, Newt. And God
> bless.

Pastor Hill leaves. Veronica turns to Newt but before she can speak…

> NEWT
> I said I was sorry. C'mon I'm being
> repentive here.

> VERONICA
> You're being a brat.

> NEWT
> Yeah, but a repentive brat.

Newt gets up, after some struggle, and makes his way back to the studio.

Veronica lingers behind then closes her eyes and says a silent prayer. Newt looks back and sees her doing this.

INT. ACCESS HOLLYWOOD SET

A HOST walks onto the set where a graphic of Newt in his radio studio can be seen on the monitors behind her.

> HOST
> Newt Richardson, the morning talk
> show host of WKAL continues to
> entertain audiences with his
> shocking Dead-air marathon. As he
> enters, what some say are the final
> days of his program, and life, we
> have exclusive interviews with his
> friends to hear what they think
> about, what many are calling a
> morbid stunt.

INTERVIEW SET - DAY

JOHN KAPLAN, a radio morning talk show host, is being interviewed for Access Hollywood.

> JOHN KAPLAN
> Honestly, I think Newt needs to
> stop. He should go home and be with
> his wife and make the best of his
> final days. In the beginning, this
> was an interesting concept, but it
> is obvious his is wearing down and
> now it is just creepy and sick.

INT. STUDIO - LATER

Newt, sits at the console with his headphones on. He sits quietly for a moment staring through the glass at Veronica who has now come out of the Green Room and faces Newt.

The "On Air" Light turns on.

> NEWT
> You know, folks, I've been
> thinking.
>   (MORE)

                    NEWT (CONT'D)
          I've sat in this chair for hours a
          day for twenty years offering
          advice, mocking injustices—and
          celebrities--telling you what's
          wrong with how you live, and
          generally spilling my guts on the
          table, and you know what? I don't
          think I've ever heeded a single
          piece of advice that a listener has
          offered me. I probably should have
          at some point, but then it's hard
          for me to take advice because I
          know everything. Nevertheless, that
          changes today. I still know
          everything. But I'm going to take
          some advice.
               (beat)
          Now, everybody who's been keeping
          score out there pull out your list
          of things to do before you die,
          write in "have a child." You heard
          me right, jot that down. And wipe
          that silly grin off your face. I'm
          going to explain.

Veronica, watching from the sound booth, looks astonished.
Newt smiles at her.

                    NEWT
          As most of you know, I've never
          been a proponent of having a child.
          But, I've done an about-face on
          this one for a couple of reasons.
          First, my wife has always wanted a
          child. And I have disappointed her
          again and again. Now, however, I am
          dying. And you know what? It scares
          me to death that I will cash my
          last check and leave my wife alone.
          Granted, she'll have a big house. A
          Mercedes convertible. An ocean
          view. But she'll have no one to
          share those things with.

Newt and Veronica make eye contact.

                    NEWT
          Basically, I leave her alone. Not
          very husbandly of me, is it? That's
          one reason I wish we had a kid.
          Second, and this one is a little
          bit egocentric, but you expect
          nothing less of me.
               (MORE)

63.

>   NEWT (CONT'D)
>   You probably don't know my wife,
>   but she's an incredibly talented
>   and smart individual. And you know
>   how rico suave I am. Basically,
>   we've wasted an incomparable gene
>   pool. Hindsight is 20/20, but our
>   kid probably would have been a
>   Harvard-educated, Nobel-prize-
>   winning world leader. First man on
>   Mars? A president? The president?
>   Discovered a cure for AIDS? Cancer?
>   He probably would have saved the
>   world. (beat) So, in fact, I stand
>   corrected, this reason is not
>   egocentric at all. My kid may have
>   saved your kid's butt in this
>   crappy world. (beat) So there you
>   have it. Two reasons to have a kid.
>   Well, actually one reason. The
>   second is just mine. (beat) Caller
>   you're on Dead Air. Speak or die.

>   CALLER 4/ VERONICA
>   Glad you came around, Newt. One
>   question, though.

>   NEWT
>   Shoot.

>   CALLER 4/ VERONICA
>   How do you know your kid would have
>   been a he?

>   NEWT
>   Well, I'm not sure that. Actually,
>   because I without a doubt have the
>   dominant genes in the family.

>   CALLER 4/ VERONICA
>   Is that so?

>   NEWT
>   Yeah, I bet even my wife would
>   agree.

He looks up at Veronica. She holds her cell-phone and smiles.

Newt laughs to himself.

>   NEWT
>   You know, caller. I'm not all sure.
>   I guess maybe I would have hoped to
>   have a son.
>   (MORE)

                         NEWT (CONT'D)
          But, no matter, if we had a girl,
          she probably would have been the
          first woman president.

Veronica enters the studio.

                         NEWT
          It's interesting, we all have
          reasons that we don't want to die,
          but I'm reminded of a story about
          P.T. Barnum, the circus king. It
          seems ol' P.T. was a bigger
          egomaniac than many claim me to be,
          and he once told a reporter that
          the thing he regretted most about
          dying was that he'd miss out on
          reading his own obituary. Too bad,
          so sad. I can't say that hold true
          for me. I'll tell ya, the thing I
          am going to regret most about being
          dead is not being able to wake up,
          roll over and see and smell my
          wife. I mean, this woman smells so
          great first thing in the morning.
          If there is such thing as sleeping
          smell, my wife possesses it.

Veronica stands across the studio looking at Newt while he
talks.

                         NEWT
          Not only that but you know how most
          of us wake up in the morning with
          that awful sour taste in our mouth?
          Well, my wife doesn't have one bad
          breath cell in her. She could sleep
          for a month and wake up with minty
          fresh breath. I'm serious. Ol' P.T.
          can regret missing his obituary,
          but I regret leaving behind the one
          good thing I have in this world.
          And there were so many things that
          I promise her; so many things that
          I never did for her that I wanted
          to. Like taking that bike ride in
          Hawaii, or buying her that ranch in
          Montana. Well, honey, you'll be
          able to afford it as soon as I'm
          gone. I hope you kept up the
          payments on my life insurance.

INTERCUT: NEWT'S VO IS HEARD AS WE CUT TO THESE VARIOUS
SCENES

INT. CAR - NIGHT

The Secretary, now in her car, listens to Newt on the radio.
She wipes a tear from her eye.

INT. BAR - NIGHT

The Construction Workers sit in a bar. Each secretly pulls
out their cell phone and call or text their spouses.

INT. HOME - NIGHT

The Jogger, at home listens to the broadcast.

When his wife enters the room, he stops her and gives her a
large hug and kiss.

BACK TO SCENE

                    NEWT
          I hope my listeners won't mind, but
          I have to take this time to
          apologize to my wife. I love her
          more then she could ever know, and
          even though I have not been the
          best of husbands I hope she will
          forgive me. I'm sorry, honey. I
          won't be able to say I'm sorry to
          everyone who deserves an apology
          from me, but honestly the only one
          that matters is you. Look, I've
          been a rotten husband for a long
          time, and I'm sorry.

                    VERONICA
          I forgive you.

                    NEWT
          Thank you. Let's take a break.
          We'll be right back after a message
          from Sunset Body Repair, where they
          can't do anything for me, but they
          can fix up that dented Yugo good as
          new.

                    REED
          We're clear.

Veronica walks over to Newt and hugs him.

                        VERONICA
              I love you so much.

                        NEWT
              I love you too. I wish I hadn't
              ruined your life.

                        VERONICA
              Newt, you didn't ruin my life.

                        NEWT
              But there was so much that you
              wanted to do. Places to go.

                        VERONICA
              Newt, I have been very happy with
              you.

                        NEWT
              I've never been able to tell you
              how happy you make me, and now, as
              I'm dying, I finally find some
              words that make sense—I hope. I
              wish I could have been there for
              you. To give you the attention and
              love you deserve. To give you kids,
              and vacations. But, I will tell you
              this, if I could, I would marry you
              again today in a second. I love
              you.

Veronica cries.

They embrace.

                        VERONICA
              I love you, Newt Richardson. Thank
              you.

Both are crying.

                        VERONICA
                    (regaining composure)
              Well, you have listeners waiting.

                        NEWT
              Yep, I guess the break is almost
              over. Hey, I have a question?

                        VERONICA
              Yeah?

                    NEWT
In the twenty years I've been doing
this show, how many times have you
called in and pretended to be a
listener?

                  VERONICA
Just once.

                    NEWT
Once?

                  VERONICA
Yeah, once. Then I became a
listener and called in every couple
of weeks.

The two smile, and she shuts the door.

INT. STUDIO - LATER

Newt sits down behind the console, places his headphones on
and pulls the microphone toward him. He wipes away the tears
and prepares to go on the air.

THE SOUND OF A TOUCH-TONE PHONE, FOLLOWED BY FOUR RINGS. AN
ANSWERING MACHINE PICKS UP:

                  MACHINE
Hello, you've reached the offices
of God. The Almighty is attending
to some duties at the moment.
Please hang up and try your call
again after the hurricane season.

                  ANNOUNCER
Counting down to dead air with the
Newt-Man on WKAL.

The "On Air" Light turns on.

                    NEWT
You know, as I sit here staring
death in the face, I have to admit
this isn't at all what I expected,
or even hoped for. We all must have
thought about how we would like to
die. I mean, our ideal death. A
fantasy death. Most would probably
choose dying in their own home, in
their own bed, saying some truly
memorable and prophetic last words.
                 (MORE)

                    NEWT (CONT'D)
But that only happens in movies.
The fact is that is not how most of
us are going out. The reality is
that we will die painfully in some
hospital of some disease we can't
pronounce. Or have a painful heart
attack and die with people we don't
know surrounding us and trying
unsuccessfully to resuscitate us.
Or maybe a car accident. Who knows.
I know for sure how I wouldn't want
to die. Burning to death. Oh man.
That has got to be the worst way I
can think of to die. How about you?
Tell me some of the ways you wish
you would or wouldn't want to die.
Hello caller, you're on the air.

                    CALLER 5
Yeah, hi Newt?

                    NEWT
Yes?

                    CALLER 5
Sorry you're dying.

                    NEWT
Thank you. Now how would you like
to die?

                    CALLER 5
I know I wouldn't want to die in a
plane crash. I can only imagine the
terror someone goes through as the
plane they're in falls out of the
sky.

                    NEWT
Yeah, that's a good one. I wouldn't
want to die that way either. The
fear would probably kill me before
the impact.

                    CALLER 5
I know right!

                    NEWT
I think it would be safe to say
that any way of dying where you are
scared and aware there is a good
probability that you will die
painfully is not good.
                    (MORE)

                    NEWT (CONT'D)
          So let's rule plane crashes out as
          an acceptable way to go. Thanks for
          your call. Next?

                    CALLER 6
          Hello? I want to die having sex.

Newt disconnects the caller.

                    NEWT
          Of course, wouldn't we all. Next!

                    CALLER 7
          Newt-Man, I want to sky dive naked
          without a parachute!

Newt disconnects the caller.

                    NEWT
          Sounds like sky diving without a
          brain. But hey. Next!

                    CALLER 8
          I know I wouldn't want to be eaten
          alive by any wild animal.

Newt disconnects the caller.

                    NEWT
          True. The only way to die by being
          eaten alive would be during sex,
          and we already covered that. One
          more!

                    CALLER 9
          I want to die of old age.

                    NEWT
          Yeah, there's always one out there
          like that. You're probably the same
          type that would ask for three more
          wishes too.

                    CALLER 9
          Sure, why not?

                    NEWT
          Why not, indeed. There you have it
          America, a quick course in ways to
          and not to die. You know I have to
          admit I have always wondered what
          it would be like to bleed to death.
                    (MORE)

                         NEWT (CONT'D)
          I mean, I'm against suicide, but
          what if you were shot or gut cut
          and instead of getting help—or
          maybe you couldn't—you just lay
          there and slowly let the blood
          drain from your body. It seems like
          you would just slowly fall asleep
          and then the end. Which, by the
          way, reminds me, ironically, I
          actually would not want to die in
          my sleep. I know that might sound
          weird. I want to know I'm dying. I
          want to face it head on and give it
          a kick in the teeth before I pass
          on. No. No passing away in the
          night for me. That truly scares me.
          I mean, how would I know I was
          dead? Looks like we have time for
          one more caller. You're on the air,
          what do you have to say?

CALLER 10 sounds shy and uncertain of her situation. She
almost seems embarrassed to be on the phone with Newt.

                    CALLER 10/ KATHERINE
          Hi Newt?

                         NEWT
          Yes, whom am I speaking with?

                    CALLER 10/ KATHERINE
          This is Katherine.

                         NEWT
          Well hello Katherine, and what are
          your thoughts about dying?

                    CALLER 10/ KATHERINE
          Well...um...I just called to
          say...Well...I think what you are
          doing on your show is good…

                         NEWT
          Thank you Katherine, I'm glad you
          approve.

                    CALLER 10/ KATHERINE
          I think your message can help a lot
          of people. You see, I'm dying too.

                         NEWT
          Really? What from?

                CALLER 10/ KATHERINE
AIDS.

                NEWT
I'd say I'm sorry but that would go
against the rules I set up for this
program, you understand.

                CALLER 10/ KATHERINE
No. Yeah, sure I understand. I
don't want sympathy or nothing. I
mean, it's my fault right?

                NEWT
Do you know how you contracted the
disease?

                CALLER 10/ KATHERINE
I have a pretty good idea. But the
reason for my call is to tell you
I'm really afraid to die. I don't
want to die!
    (begins crying)

                NEWT
Katherine, how old are you?

                CALLER 10/ KATHERINE
Fifteen.

                NEWT
    (off the air to himself
     and his staff)
Jeez.
    (back on air)
Katherine, do your parents know you
called me?

                CALLER 10/ KATHERINE
I don't live with them anymore. I
ran away two years ago.

                NEWT
And how far along are you with the
AIDS virus?

                CALLER 10/ KATHERINE
My T-cells have been dropping for
the past three months, I just got
over a case of strep throat, but
now the doctors think I have
pneumonia. I have to go to the
clinic tomorrow for tests. Newt, I
don't want to go.
              (MORE)

                    CALLER 10/ KATHERINE (CONT'D)
I don't want them to tell me I'm
going to die soon. What it they
won't let me leave because they say
I'm too sick? I don't want to stay
in a hospital.

                    NEWT
I don't blame you. There is no
worse place to get well than a
hospital. But Katherine, I don't
think they can make you stay. You
can refuse treatment. There are
many AIDS patients who go home for
their final days. You sound strong.

                    CALLER 10/ KATHERINE
Well I feel okay now, but every day
I wake up scared of what might
happen that day. I'm too scared to
go outside in case I catch a cold
or something.

                    NEWT
Katherine, remember what I said at
the start of this show? Life is to
be lived. I know you're scared.
Hell, I'm not too excited about
what's going to happen to me next,
but you can't live the rest of your
life locked away in your apartment.
That's not living.

                    CALLER 10/ KATHERINE
I know, I know, but...

                    NEWT
No, there are no "buts" here, the
game we're playing doesn't accept
them. It's black and white, win or
lose, on or off. Katherine I know
this is rough, especially for
someone as young as you, but you
have to fight your fear. You know
there are some support groups for
people in your situation, and maybe
you can find a group and get some
help or at least find some friends
that have this in common with you.
Stay on the line Katherine and
we'll get you some numbers okay.

                    CALLER 10/ KATHERINE
Okay. Thanks Newt.

                              NEWT
                    You take care kid and I'll see ya
                    on the other side. We'll take a
                    break and be back in a minute.

A PROMO plays.

THE SOUND OF A TOUCH-TONE PHONE, FOLLOWED BY FOUR RINGS. AN
ANSWERING MACHINE PICKS UP

                              MACHINE
                    Hello. You've reached the offices
                    of God. Normal business hours are
                    from nine a.m. to five p.m.
                    Heavenly Standard Time. All our
                    operators are busy assisting other
                    sinners at this time. Please hold
                    or try our Automated Forgiveness
                    Information Line. If you're calling
                    to pray for the health of a family
                    member or friend, press one. If
                    you're calling to pray for the
                    health of a pet, press two. If
                    you're calling to pray about the
                    Super Bowl, take the Steelers minus
                    seven.

                              ANNOUNCER
                    You're all going to Hell for
                    listening. The Newt-Man on WKAL.

Newt pushes back from the console and runs his hands over his
face.

Newt sits quietly while his assistants and show producers
busy themselves around him.

There is a buzz of activity but it is all a blur to Newt who,
though sitting there looking at the people talking to him and
watching what is going on, is not really comprehending what
they are saying. He is detached from the situation as if in a
daydream, until finally they cue him to go back on the air.

The "On Air" light turns on.

                              NEWT
                    We're back. Let's take a call.
                    Who's on the other side of this
                    line?

                              CALLER 11
                    Hello.

                    NEWT
It's the Newt-Man. Who's this?

                    CALLER 11
Yeah, this is Carl.

                    NEWT
What's on your mind, Carl?

                    CALLER 11
I was wondering what crossed your
mind right when you found out that
you would die. What does it feel
like when the doctor says there's
nothing more he can do?

                    NEWT
Well, it doesn't feel good, I'll
tell you that much. Basically, for
me, I felt trapped. Helpless. Out
of control. When I was 12 years
old, growing up in Northern Jersey.
One day coming home from school, a
couple of friends and I walked past
these three apple trees behind a
neighbor's backyard shed. The
apples were rotting and falling to
the ground. Well, we just couldn't
resist throwing some of them. We
tossed a few at a telephone pole,
and before you knew it we were
pelting this pristine white shed
with them. For about a half-hour.
Splat. Bam. I don't know if I
thought I was going to get away
with it. But, as you might suspect,
I didn't. I was in my room that
evening when I heard the doorbell.
It was Mr. Blackburn, owner of the
shed. I overheard him relay the
story to my parents—one of my
friends had ratted on me. My
parents were livid. And I heard my
dad coming down the hall. I was in
trouble. There was nothing I could
do. Nowhere I could go. I was
trapped. When the doctor told me
that I was terminal, I got the same
feeling. No way out. Soon, I was
able to handle it. And before I
knew it, I was handling it well.
(beat) Caller, you sound like a
young man, have you ever had anyone
close to you die?

                    CALLER 11
          My grandfather. But we weren't that
          close.

                    NEWT
          Do you know what his death was
          like?

                    CALLER 11
          He had cancer and lung disease and
          cirrhosis of the liver and who
          knows what else.

                    NEWT
          Old man?

                    CALLER 11
          73.

                    NEWT
          Was he at home?

                    CALLER 11
          The hospital.

                    NEWT
          So it was expected?

                    CALLER 11
          Sort of, I guess. It was kind of
          weird. On the day he died, he had
          something to tell my grandmother.
          He asked the nurses to call her
          several times. They tried, but she
          was with my parents. They finally
          got through, but by the time
          Grandma got there he was gone.

                    NEWT
          He knew he was going to die.

                    CALLER 11
          That's what Grandma says.

                    NEWT
          That seems to be another phase of
          the process—at least for some
          people. I felt trapped when the
          doctor first told me. But later, a
          few days later, I realized that I
          sort of knew it was coming. Or at
          least I wasn't as surprised as I
          thought I should be.

>   CALLER 11
>   That's reassuring.

>   NEWT
>   Sure. Let's hope we all can develop
>   such a peace.

>   CALLER 11
>   You know, my grandma still wonders
>   what Grandpa wanted to tell her.

>   NEWT
>   Who knows? But if I were your
>   grandmother, I'd be checking the
>   crevices in the basement for cash.

Newt gives Reed the signal that he needs a break and he takes off his headset.

Newt is the weakest he has been. Every movement is a struggle. He looks tired, pale, weak. Newt sits at the console staring into space.

>   ANNOUNCER VO
>   Run for your lives; it's an
>   earthquake. Never mind. It's just
>   the Newt-Man on WKAL.

INT. JOE FOSTER'S OFFICE - MORNING

Charles sits in Joe's office with two other executives, MICHAEL BRATTON and KEITH STERNAN.

>   CHARLES
>   So, I see they sent in the cavalry.
>   One executive vice president and
>   the president.

>   JOE
>   We have a serious situation here,
>   Charles. You know that. It's not
>   like Newt's typical antics. He is
>   literally dying on the air. We're
>   all concerned.

>   MICHAEL BRATTON
>   He is weak. It's sad.

>   KEITH STERNAN
>   Pathetic.

                    CHARLES
Don't you guys worry about Newt. He
can handle himself. Sure, he looks
weak. But when the light goes on,
he's on the mark. He's a pro.

                    JOE
It goes beyond that, Charles. We're
also concerned that leaving him on
the air could jeopardize the
integrity of the station.

                    CHARLES
Just employing Newt jeopardizes the
station's integrity. I mean, come
on.

                    MICHAEL BRATTON
Charles, right now, we are the
laughing stock of the broadcasting
industry. Entertainment Tonight,
Access Hollywood, CNN, Fox News,
they are all blasting us for
keeping Newt on the air. Bill
O'Riely called Newt a Pinhead last
night on his Pinhead and Patriots
bits. We're getting slammed.

                    KEITH STERNAN
And you know very well that the
syndicates are a bit skittish. Some
advertisers have cancelled.

                    CHARLES
I know. A couple.

                    JOE
It wasn't an easy decision,
Charles. But we've decided to pull
the plug.

                    CHARLES
What? You can't. Gentlemen, I don't
know how you can even consider
pulling the plug on this show. Newt
has the biggest audience he has
ever had and you are making the
most money you have ever made off
of him.

                    MICHAEL BRATTON
We have to, Charles. The future of
the station is at stake.

                    CHARLES
This is the future of the station.
Newt made this station what it is,
and now he's setting us up for the
next century. Ten years from now,
we'll look back and realize that
this marathon put WKAL on the map.

                    MICHAEL BRATTON
This is not the type of publicity
we welcome.

                    CHARLES
Robert, we logged 350 calls in the
past hour alone. People can't get
through, the lines are clogged. Our
listeners are responding. A fan
site on Facebook was set up two
days ago and already has half-a-
million fans. The people love the
show. Screw the critics.

The three executive looks at each other questioningly.

                    CHARLES (CONT'D)
What did you gentlemen expect? This
is ground-breaking radio.

                    JOE
The only ground we're breaking is
the grave we're digging for
ourselves. This has to stop. It's a
circus. We're accomplishing
nothing.

                    CHARLES
Nothing, you say? Nothing? Tell
that to the 15-year-old-girl with
AIDS we just put in touch with a
support group. This program was the
impetus she needed to reach out.
And it's going to do the same for
hundreds of listeners. (beat) But
even if she is the only person we
touch through this program, it
would be worth it. What if she were
your kid, Joe? Robert?

                    JOE
That's hardly fair, Charles.

                    CHARLES
          And as far as the syndicates and
          advertisers, let the cream rise to
          the top. Some will stay—and will be
          thankful they did. Those that leave
          will regret it. We've already had a
          couple of stations come back on-
          line. And we've signed up at least
          ten new ones for tomorrow. I'm not
          worried about losing
          advertisers—we'll still show a
          profit.

                    JOE
          Yeah, but...

                    CHARLES
          No buts, Joe. You promised you
          would keep us on until you were
          losing money. Well, you're not.
          Only courage. I won't be the one to
          tell Newt it's over. If you want
          him off, you'll have to do it
          yourself.

Charles gets up and opens the door.

                    CHARLES
          How can you pull the plug on the
          man who put that suit on your back,
          Joe? The man who paid for your
          castle in Malibu, Jeffery? We owe
          it to him. Now, excuse me, I have a
          show to produce.

Charles storms out of the room.

INT. GREEN ROOM - DAY

Newt looks the worse for wear. Dark rings are under his eyes.
He is pale and gaunt and his clothes drape off his body. His
dry cough is worse and he can barely speak a complete
sentence without coughing.

Reed enters the room.

                    REED
          You ready to go on Newt?

Veronica holds Newt's hand and steadies him as he sits on the
couch.

Newt's body shakes. He doesn't respond to Reed.

                    VERONICA
          No just yet Freddy. Can you give us
          another few minutes.

                    REED
          Sure, Mrs. Richardson, I still have
          a number of carts with best of bits
          I can play. Take your time.

                    VERONICA
          Thank you.

Reed leaves and Veronica sits on the couch next to Newt.

                    VERONICA
          You know, you've had a good run,
          and the show has been great, why
          don't we call it quits and get you
          home?

                    NEWT
          No! I can't quit now. I need to
          finish this thing.

                    VERONICA
          But why? I don't understand why you
          want to rush the inevitable. At
          home I could take care of you and
          you might have a little longer.

                    NEWT
          Veronica, I don't want to have any
          longer.

Charles steps up in the background unbeknownst to Newt.

                    NEWT
          My entire body feels like it's
          giving up the ghost, which I guess
          it is actually (laughs and coughs).
          I really, just want to finish my
          show and know my last words will be
          heard by millions of people. Is
          that okay?

                    VERONICA
          Yes, of course, but you have to let
          me worry about you, it's what I do
          best.

Newt smiles. Then as if he knew Charles was there and without
turning...

                    NEWT
          And how about you, Charles, what
          are you going to do?

Charles walks over and kneels down to face Newt, putting his
hand on Newt's shoulder, upon which Newt places his own hand
and squeezes.

                    CHARLES
          I'm going to watch my friend give
          the best swan song in radio
          history.

                    NEWT
          Does that mean were staying on?

                    CHARLES
          Everything's taken care of. I told
          the suits they were making more
          money off your death than they ever
          did while you were alive and they
          responded quite well to that. Do
          not be surprised to see a couple of
          paramedics come into the station,
          though. Foster wanted them here for
          insurance reasons. When you go they
          need to at least make an attempt to
          save you. Ironic isn't it,
          management has been trying to kill
          your show for years and now when it
          is finally coming to an end they
          have to try their best to keep you
          alive.

                    NEWT
          I always knew I would have the last
          laugh.

Charles stands to leave and Newt grabs his hand. Charles
stops and looks at his friend.

                    NEWT (CONT'D)
          There's one more thing you can do
          for me buddy.

Newt hands Charles a business card.

DREAM SEQUENCE

It is dark. SOFT, RHYTHMIC MUSIC. Slowly a bright white light
can be seen in the distance down the long dark tunnel.

Newt drifts toward the light. As he approaches a figure can just barely be seen in the light. The figure beckons for Newt to come closer.

As if from miles away, Veronica and Charles CALL Newt's name.

> VERONICA
> Newt. Newt.

> CHARLES
> Newt. Wake up buddy. You have a
> show to do.

INT. RADIO STUDIO - LATER

Newt sits in his seat in the studio.

Everyone watches, as Veronica and Charles try to revive him from his catatonic state.

Veronica has to place the headset on Newt's head since he fumbles with the cord.

As Veronica and Charles begin to leave, Newt holds Veronica's hand.

> NEWT
> Stay.

Charles brings her a chair to sit on next to Newt, where she sits and holds his shaking hand.

Newt has an uncontrollable hacking cough for a moment.

Laura and Reed look at each other concerned. Laura is crying. Reed hugs her.

In the listening area, Pastor Hill stands watching from the listening area.

Newt pulls himself together and, before Charles can leave, calls out to him.

> NEWT
> Hey, Chuck. Thank you.

> CHARLES
> Thank you, Newt.

Charles walks out of the studio and down the hall before Newt can say anything else.

Veronica smiles at Newt.

>   VERONICA
>   He always was your friend, you
>   know.
>
>   NEWT
>   Yeah. The best friend I could hope
>   for.

Reed cues Newt to go on the air.

Veronica sits at his side holding his hand.

>   NEWT
>   Well folks, I believe the final
>   hours are upon us, do if I am going
>   to do anything profound I guess I
>   had better do it now. Throughout
>   this process of dying I have been a
>   bit reflective on my life--as great
>   as it was--and life in general.
>   While I was not a great
>   practitioner of this--as my lovely
>   wife will attest--I have come to
>   this conclusion: Life is about
>   love.

Newt looks over at Pastor Hill, who gives Newt a thumbs-up
sign and a smile.

Veronica smiles to Pastor Hill and squeezes Newt's hand. She
fights back tears.

>   NEWT (CONT'D)
>   I ask you, and leave this with you
>   to contemplate after I am gone,
>   what is the sole purpose for you
>   being placed on the blue ball we
>   call earth was to love. Love each
>   other. Love yourself. Love
>   everyone. Even those idiots in
>   Washington and the Middle East.

INTERCUT: NEWT'S VO OVER THESE VARIOUS SCENES

INT. OFFICE - DAY

The Secretary listens on her Internet radio and she hugs a co-
worker who walks past.

EXT. CONSTRUCTION SITE - DAY

The Construction Workers are bumping fists while listening to
Newt on a small radio.

BACK TO SCENE

                    NEWT (CONT'D)
          What if we cared for others ore
          than we cared for ourselves? How
          would the world be different? I
          know, I lived my life the exact
          opposite of what I am saying now,
          but that is why I can speak with
          authority on this subject. I was
          wrong. Yes folks, record that, mark
          your calendars. The Newt-man for
          the first time ever on radio has
          admitted he was wrong about
          something. I have never said that
          before, and trust me, never will
          again, but I screwed up and had it
          all bass-ackwards. Lennon and
          McCartney had it right, all you
          need is love. Richard Bach wrote
          some great books about it. Others
          as well. What if we just stopped
          hating and starting loving. It is
          idealistic I know, but it is not as
          difficult as we make it. Just start
          today. Let someone have the right
          away when you drive. Open the door
          for someone at the store. Love the
          one you are with. Love your enemy.
          Love each other. Honk if you want
          to love more than you hate.

Newt leans over and kisses Veronica and whispers:

                    NEWT
          I love you.

Veronica cries and she mouths it back.

                    NEWT (CONT'D)
          Alright enough of that, let me tell
          you something else I discovered,
          death is a lonely business. You
          would think that people would want
          to come by one last time to say
          good-bye, but no. No, they would
          rather wait until you're dead then
          say things about you.
                    (MORE)

                              NEWT (CONT'D)
          And I don't blame people. I mean,
          what do you say to a living corpse
          on time share? It's got to be
          uncomfortable. I wouldn't know what
          to say and I get paid to talk. Do
          you ask how a dying person is
          doing? Do you ask what they have
          planned for tomorrow? No, I don't
          blame my friends for not coming by
          to see me off. It's okay. I've got
          my wife and my radio family.

INTERCUT: NEWT'S VO IS HEARD AS WE CUT TO:

INT. CHARLES' OFFICE - DAY

Charles sits behind his desk listening to Newt's broadcast.
Tears have filled his eyes and he sits quietly, staring off
into space as he listens.

BACK TO SCENE

                              NEWT (CONT'D)
          I know it's hard on them and I
          truly appreciate what they are
          going through now to allow me this
          last selfish pleasure. I thank God
          for kind people like these. In
          closing...

Laura and Reed are surprised.

There is suddenly a bit of frantic action in the studio.

Charles and Joe have come to the studio window to look in on
Newt.

Veronica stares at Newt as he clinches her hand tighter.

Newt smiles and winks.

                              NEWT (CONT'D)
          I took the time to write some thank
          you's. I hope you all will indulge
          this dying man's last request to
          read them to you now. It would seem
          "now" might be all there is. I want
          to thank my staff for all the years
          of great work.
                              (MORE)

>   NEWT (CONT'D)
>   If it wasn't for them I certainly
>   would not be on the air sounding
>   even reasonably coherent.

ON REED

>   NEWT (CONT'D)
>   Thanks to Freddy, my engineer
>   extraordinaire. Without your wiring
>   wizadry I'd just be a shlep with a
>   dead mike. Something my wife has
>   complained about for years.

ON LAURA

>   NEWT (CONT'D)
>   To my assistant, Laura, for her
>   hard work and undying patience with
>   me.

TO NEWT IN THE STUDIO

>   NEWT (CONT'D)
>   To the volunteers who answer the
>   phones, thank you for all your
>   time. Thanks guys for all the help
>   and for making an old man sound
>   good.

Newt coughs uncontrollably.

Veronica finishes reading his note.

Newt slumps over and rests his head on her shoulder. He is
still conscious but very weak.

With tears streaming down her cheeks, Veronica chokes out
these final words.

ON STUDIO WINDOW WHERE JOE STANDS

>   VERONICA
>   To Joe Foster, who with any luck
>   will die of a heart attack when he
>   hears that I am thanking him. To
>   you Joe, for having the balls to
>   keep me on the air all these years,
>   even against your better judgment.
>   To Charles, my friend, my partner,
>   my champion.
>   (MORE)

                    VERONICA (CONT'D)
          For putting up with all my crap and
          still doing a job that no one else
          could do better.

ON VERONICA IN THE STUDIO

                    VERONICA (CONT'D)
          And finally, to my wife, for the
          best wife I could ever hope to
          have. She has been more than a
          friend and a lover even when I fell
          short on my end. I will love you
          always and forever.
          Goodnight...good morning, whatever
          time it is right now. Take care
          people and I'll see ya all on the
          other side. God bless.

Newt leans up to kiss Veronica on her forehead then, as he
tries to push away from the console, he slips from his chair
and falls onto the floor.

                    VERONICA (CONT'D)
          Newt!

Charles, watches through the window, aghast.

The paramedics rush in to tend to Newt.

When the paramedics try to remove Veronica from the
situation, Charles stops them.

Veronica stays and holds Newt's hand.

Reed and Laura watch in horror.

INTERCUT: THE SOUNDS FROM THE STUDIO CAN BE HEARD

INT. CAR - DAY

The Business Man listens as he drives. Shocked. He turns the
radio up.

INT. OFFICE - DAY

The Secretary cries while she listens.

Many of her co-workers have gathered around her desk to
listen as well. Many of them are crying also.

EXT. CONSTRUCTION SITE - DAY

The Construction Workers have stopped working and are
listening intently to the radio.

EXT. JOG PATH - DAY

The Jogger stops running. He cups his hands over his ears to
listen.

BACK TO SCENE

Paramedics try to resuscitate Newt with a defibrillator.

                         PARAMEDIC
              Clear.

The first attempt to resuscitate Newt fails and the
paramedics trying again. The second and third attempts fail
as well.

Charles hold Veronica who cries.

Pastor Hill also consuls Veronica.

Joe enters and turns off the broadcast signal.

At that moment, the switch to the microphone is turned off
and there is only "dead-air," or silence.

In SILENCE the paramedics try without success to revive Newt.

OS the faint sound OF CARS HONKING.

The HONKING INCREASES IN VOLUME as hundreds of car and truck
horns enter the chorus.

The sound BRIDGES to the next scene and fades to the RHYTHMIC
HEAVENLY CHORUS we have heard before in the...

DREAM SEQUENCE

As in the other DREAM SEQUENCES, hovering over Newt's
shoulder, he floats down a dark tunnel with a bright white
light at the end.

The faint form of a man can just be seen inside the light but
he is never fully seen. The RHYTHMIC MUSIC raises to a
crescendo as Newt finally reaches the light.

After seemingly considering it for a moment, Newt proceeds to
step into the light and disappears. The white light
intensifies and BURNS OUT the scene.

FADE OUT.

LOGLINE

After disastrous reviews of his latest exhibition, an artist questions his talent, diving into a tailspin of self-doubt and reflection which affects his personal and professional relationships, and only through deep introspection and study is he able to attempt a rebound.

<u>ART LIFE</u>

Written by

Douglas King

FADE IN:

INT. APARTMENT - NIGHT

SCOTT MARTIN (late 40s), middle-aged, but wearing it well,
enters the apartment with a bang. He is drunk. He is happy.

                         SCOTT
               That was great. That was great,
               right?

Entering the apartment behind Scott, ANNA KINGSBY (40s), self-
assured, projecting confidence and control, closes the door
and tosses her coat on a console nearby.

                         ANNA
               Yes, sweetie, it was great. I think
               people really enjoyed it.

                         SCOTT
               You're sure?

Scott, pours himself a drink from the bar cart.

The room is well appointed in Bohemian chic. Art canvases
lean against most surfaces. Some are finished, others in
various states of completion. All of the paintings look very
similar.

                         ANNA
               You sure you need another drink?

Scott pours a second glass and hands it to Anna.

                         SCOTT
               Need? Debatable. Want? Definitely!

Anna sits on the sofa.

She kicks off her shoes and curls her legs under her. She
sips her drink. Bourbon, neat.

                         ANNA
               Relax. I think it went very well.

Scott stares at one of his unfinished canvases.

                         SCOTT
               I hope so.

Anna watches Scott.

                    ANNA
          Come here.

Anna beckons Scott to sit down next to her.

Scott walks over to the sofa. He downs his drink in one gulp.

                    SCOTT
          Let me refill.

Anna reaches for him.

                    ANNA
          No. I need you able to perform.

Anna pulls Scott down onto her. She kisses him.

Scott stops again.

                    SCOTT
          Maybe I should call Brett? Ask him
          what he thinks.

                    ANNA
          Is that really what you want to
          discuss right now?

Anna stands and walks away in as sexy a fashion as is humanly possible. Her walk alone would finish most virgins.

Along the way she unzips her dress slowly. Seductively. Never revealing anything.

                    ANNA (CONT'D)
          I think I'll go to bed.

Scott watches.

Anna, exits the room. A moment later her dress flies through the door, landing on the floor.

Scott, with the speed of a jaguar, moves to get to the bedroom.

GIGGLING AND KISSING emanate from the bedroom.

INT. APARTMENT - KITCHEN - LATER

Scott sits at the breakfast table, sipping a mug of tea while reading the newspaper.

Anna enters.

3.

She puts the kettle on and prepares a cup of tea for herself.

                    ANNA
          And how are we this morning?

                    SCOTT
          On my third cup of tea. Unfocused.
          Unsettled. Underfed.

                    ANNA
          Ahhh. Pour baby. If you hadn't kept
          me up so late, I would've made
          breakfast sooner. You only have
          yourself to blame.

                    SCOTT
          I can't help that I perform like a
          porn star.

                    ANNA
          You're such a romantic.

Anna fetches eggs and bacon from the refrigerator and begins
to prepare breakfast.

                    SCOTT
          Well, thank you.

                    ANNA
          Of course, a true romantic would
          have made me breakfast in bed.

Scott realizes his shortcoming.

                    SCOTT
          I'm sorry, I --

                    ANNA
          I'm kidding.

Scott resumes reading the paper. Anna watches him.

                    ANNA (CONT'D)
          You're still stressed about the
          show?

                    SCOTT
          I haven't had a sale in nearly a
          year.

Anna crosses to Scott and rubs his shoulders.

                    ANNA
          Have you heard from Brett yet?

                         SCOTT
               We texted. He's coming by.

                         ANNA
               He didn't say anything?

                         SCOTT
               Nope.

Anna reacts surprised. She returns to the kitchen to continue
food prep.

                         ANNA
               I'm sure it's all good.

Scott puts down the paper. He turns to Anna.

                         SCOTT
               If it was all good, don't you think
               he would have said something?

Scott stands and cross the room. Anna watches.

                         SCOTT (CONT'D)
               I feel like a man on death row.
                    (exaggerated)
               Dead man walking!

                         ANNA
               I'm glad you're not being overly
               dramatic.

                         SCOTT
               You realize that if I get a bad
               review that could be it for me?

                         ANNA
               I don't think that's true. Wait til
               Brett gets here before you write
               your obituary.

                         SCOTT
               If the show went well, Brett would
               have said something in his text.

                         ANNA
               Or, it went so well, he wants to
               share the news in person.

Anna crosses again and soothes Scott.

                         ANNA (CONT'D)
               Either way, we'll get through this.
               We always have and always will.

They kiss.

INT. APARTMENT STUDIO - MORNING

Scott sits in front of his easel. An unfinished canvas in front of him. He sips tea from a mug.

He picks up his paint brush and begins working the canvas.

He works in fits of stops and starts. Each time stepping back to stare at the marks he made.

His expression is one of frustration.

Scott squeezes more paint on his palette and mixes it.

He selects a different brush and applies the paint in quick squiggly strokes. He works the entire canvas with frantic movements.

After a flurry of motion he stops, steps back and stares at what he has done.

He throws the brush at the canvas and walks away.

INT. APARTMENT - STUDIO - DAY

Scott sits in a worn but comfortable chair with his sketch book.

The painting has been tossed to the side. A blank canvas stands dauntingly in its place on the easel.

BRETT TOMKINS (30s), a sharp dressed and tongued man, enters. He is all smiles and graciousness. He is not a used car salesman but only a few rungs up the evolutionary ladder.

Scott sees him and stands. The two hug a proud man hug.

                    BRETT
          Glad to see you made it home safe
          last night. You tied one on.

                    SCOTT
          I wasn't embarrassing was I?

                    DRUTT
          No more than usual.

Scott reacts shocked.

>   BRETT (CONT'D)
>   Man, Anna was right, you're wound
>   tight.
>
>   SCOTT
>   When did you talk with Anna?
>
>   BRETT
>   She let me in your home. Scott,
>   c'mon, man. Do you need a joint to
>   relax?
>
>   SCOTT
>   Wouldn't hurt.
>
>   BRETT
>   Now you're talking.
>   (beat)
>   You have any?
>
>   SCOTT
>   I just might.

Scott looks around in his various cabinets.

Brett looks at the canvases stacked around the studio.

Scott finds a joint. He holds it up triumphantly.

>   BRETT
>   Awesome! Light 'er up!

Scott sits in his comfy chair, locates a lighter and hits the
joint.

He passes it to Brett, who waves him away.

>   BRETT (CONT'D)
>   Sorry man, I've got to go to the
>   gallery. I can't be stoned. But you
>   definitely need it.

Scott looks at Brett amazed and surprised.

>   SCOTT
>   Was last night so bad?
>
>   BRETT
>   I wouldn't say so bad, but --
>
>   SCOTT
>   It was bad.

                    BRETT
          It was a bit more than the opposite
          of good.

                    SCOTT
          Shit, Brett, just tell me the
          truth.

Brett sits on the edge of a table in front of Scott.

                    BRETT
          Look, you're in a rut right now --

                    SCOTT
          Apparently I have been for awhile.

Brett shrugs, not disagreeing.

                    BRETT
          Sure, but all ruts end. We've
          discussed this, what do critics
          know?

Scott looks up, surprised.

                    BRETT (CONT'D)
          You haven't read the reviews? I
          thought --

                    SCOTT
          Son of a bitch, Brett! Do you have
          any good news?

                    BRETT
          You have a smoking hot girlfriend
          who loves you very much.

                    SCOTT
          About my art!

Anna enters.

Scott stubs out the joint.

                    BRETT
          Scott, buddy. It's going to be
          fine.

Scott stands. He kicks a hole in a canvas.

                    BRETT (CONT'D)
          Well, that canvas won't, but there
          are so many that will be.

                    ANNA
          Scott --

                    SCOTT
          Did you know about this? About the
          reviews?

Anna looks down.

                    SCOTT (CONT'D)
          Shit! How bad?

                    BRETT
          When have we ever listened to
          reviews? You do what you do. Screw
          them.

                    ANNA
          Honey, you paint for you, not for
          reviews. What's it matter?

                    SCOTT
          It matters because if reviews are
          negative, then collectors don't
          buy. If collectors don't buy, then
          we don't have money and Brett
          decides to hang other artists who
          will make him money.

Brett shrugs. He agrees.

                    ANNA
          Brett won't do that to you.

Brett smiles an insincere smile.

                    SCOTT
          Let me read one.

                    BRETT
          I don't see the point...

                    SCOTT
          Brett, let me read one of the damn
          reviews.

Brett looks at Anna for help.

                    SCOTT (CONT'D)
          Why, are you looking at her? Fine,
          I'll find it myself.

Scott takes his cell phone and starts searching.

Brett stands and takes the phone away.

> BRETT
> Listen, buddy, reading the review
> won't do you any good. Here's the
> thing, they say your work has
> become stale. That you haven't
> broken new ground in some time and
> that your derivative of yourself.

> SCOTT
> How is that possible? How can one's
> own work be derivative of itself?

> BRETT
> I don't know, I don't write that
> shit, I just deal with the fallout.

> ANNA
> So, you start exploring some new
> motifs. You've been working in the
> same style for awhile.

> SCOTT
> You agree? You think I'm in a rut
> too?

> BRETT
> Not really helping me.

Anna shrugs.

> SCOTT
> Shit.
> (beat)
> Shit. Shit. Shit.

Scott lights the joint again and takes another hit.

> ANNA
> I don't think --

Brett shoots Anna a look to be quiet.

> BRETT
> So this show didn't go our way.
> We'll do another.

> SCOTT
> Another of the same derivative
> shit!?

> BRETT
> No. You paint some new shit.

Scott stops and stares at Brett. Brett points at the joint in Scott's hand.

                    BRETT (CONT'D)
          I'm joking man. That's stuffs not
          helping like I thought it would.
          You sure it's still good?

                    ANNA
          Brett! Stop enabling him!

                    BRETT
          Scott, man, this is not the end of
          the world. We'll come back from
          this. The collectors will come
          back. You just need to find your
          mojo again. Dig deep. Maybe lay off
          that stuff.

Brett points to the joint.

Scott gives him a dirty look.

                    BRETT (CONT'D)
          Or not. Whatever. It's your method.

                    ANNA
               (sarcastically)
          Thanks for coming by Brett. You
          were a great help.

Brett realizes he is dismissed.

                    BRETT
          Always my pleasure.
               (beat)
          Seriously, I'm putting another show
          on the calendar in a few months.
          Will that work?

                    SCOTT
          I don't know, Brett. Maybe I'm
          done.

                    BRETT
          What are you talking about, done?
          You're never done, man. You're an
          artist. It's in your blood. You
          paint to live and live to paint.

                    SCOTT
          I'll think about it.

                    BRETT
          Let me know. It's going to all work
          out. Trust me. Big solo show. Your
          rebirth. Like a phoenix --

                    ANNA
          We'll call you.

                    BRETT
          I'm telling you man, it's going to
          be great. Now, get to work!

Brett exits.

Scott flops into his comfy chair. He reaches for the joint
but Anna stops him and stubs it out.

                    ANNA
          You don't need that.

                    SCOTT
          I need something. Apparently I'm
          derivative of myself.

                    ANNA
          Maybe you are. So what.

Scott looks at her questioningly.

Anna sits on the edge of his chair.

                    ANNA (CONT'D)
          All great artists have periods.
          This period is coming to an end. We
          are putting a period on this
          period.

                    SCOTT
          I may be too stoned to understand
          you.

                    ANNA
          What matters is you stop looking
          back and start looking forward.

                    SCOTT
          If I knew how to do that, don't you
          think I would have already?

                    ANNA
          Would you?

                    SCOTT
          What are you saying?

                      ANNA
            Scott, you've been living off your
            work for years, the work that made
            you who you are, but I think you're
            afraid to try something new because
            maybe you're worried the love will
            go away.

Scott can't look her in the eye.

                  ANNA (CONT'D)
            Guess what? The love is going away.

Scott looks at her now.

                  ANNA (CONT'D)
            Not from me. Your collectors.

                  SCOTT
            What do they expect from me?

                  ANNA
            Who are you painting for? Yourself?
            The critics?

Scott looks around at his unfinished canvases.

                  ANNA (CONT'D)
            I know you've been feeling it too.
            Look at all this work you can't
            finish. You know why? You don't
            even like it yourself any more.
            Tell me the truth, when was the
            last time you were excited to come
            in here and work?

Scott sits silently.

                  ANNA (CONT'D)
            That's what I thought. Your
            collectors want to see the
            excitement you had when you
            started. That passion that drove
            you. Find that again and they'll
            all be back.

Anna kisses Scott and smiles at him. He hugs her.

INT. APARTMENT STUDIO - NIGHT

Scott sits in his comfy chair surrounded by unfinished work,
easels, paint tubes, palettes, sketchbooks, basically a
cliche artist studio.

He looks at the various canvases leaning against every surface and the dried paint. Dried paint brushes. Dried, empty bottles of whiskey.

Dry.

A paint splattered CD player sits on a cabinet. CD cases litter the shelf around it.

Scott stands and picks through the CDs until he finds one that interests him.

He puts it in the player.

The music begins and Scott sets to cleaning the studio.

SERIES OF SHOTS

- Scott organizes all of his tubes of paint. Puts them in rows based on color. He throws away dried tubes.

- Scott organizes brushes. Cleans them. Throws some away. Places them in jars.

- Scott gathers the various loose pieces of paper with rough sketch and his sketch books. He stacks them in an orderly fashion.

- Scott stacks the canvases. Some he wipes cleans of the paint that is on them.

When the music stops, the studio is completely organized.

Scott is pleased with what he has accomplished. An organized space. An organized mind.

Anna enters. She is immediately taken aback by the clean look.

She smiles at Scott, who smiles back.

INT. APARTMENT - KITCHEN

Anna and Scott sit together at the dinner table. A nice meal before them. She drinks a glass of wine. He, a glass of bourbon.

                    SCOTT
          Marden once said, what he liked
          about abstract expressionism was
          that it didn't pay to get terribly
          analytical about it.
                    (MORE)

                    SCOTT (CONT'D)
          That it was better if you just went
          with the painting.

                    ANNA
          I agree.

                    SCOTT
          I wish the critics did.

                    ANNA
          Don't let them get in your head.
          Paint what comes from here --

Anna points to Scott's forehead.

                    ANNA (CONT'D)
          And here.

Anna points to Scott's chest.

                    ANNA (CONT'D)
          That's what you've always done.
          That's what attracted me to you.

                    SCOTT
          And all this time I thought it was
          my rugged good looks and charm.

                    ANNA
          One out of two isn't bad.

                    SCOTT
          Hey!
               (beat)
          Wait, which one?

                    ANNA
          Focus on the fact you're batting
          five hundred.

Scott lifts his drink glass and the two click glasses.

                    ANNA (CONT'D)
          The studio looks amazing.

                    SCOTT
          If I'm starting new then the space
          better look new.

The two eat in silence for a moment.

                    ANNA
          I was thinking. Maybe we should get
          away for the weekend. Drive to the
          Hill Country.

                    SCOTT
          Can you get away?

                    ANNA
          Sure. I just completed work on the
          Morris account. I have some time
          before they need me again and
          before I start work for that
          restaurant opening.

                    SCOTT
          A little r and r from pr.

                    ANNA
          It's good to be the boss sometimes.

                    SCOTT
          I'll make some arrangements.
             (beat)
          You remember the last time we got
          away?

                    ANNA
          New Orleans? We visited every
          gallery, but you made up for it by
          buying me this lovely necklace.

Anna fingers a beautiful necklace she wears.

                    SCOTT
          I totally forgot about that trip. I
          was thinking about California. We
          stayed near the beach. The light
          was amazing.

                    ANNA
          That was a great trip too. What
          about it?

                    SCOTT
          I was just thinking how perfect it
          was to be away from the stress of
          producing and being able to
          spending time with you. I love you.

                    ANNA
          I love you too. What's made you so
          reflective all of a sudden?

                    SCOTT
          I know I can be difficult to be
          around sometimes --

                    ANNA
          Sometimes?

Scott grimaces.

                    SCOTT
          I just want you to know I recognize
          it and I appreciate you. You've
          always been good for me.

                    ANNA
          That's so true. Everyone says so.

                    SCOTT
          Wow. A dig for a compliment. Can I
          take back what I said?

                    ANNA
          Nope. Too late. It's out in the
          universe.

Scott takes a bite of food.

                    SCOTT
          What if I'm washed up?

                    ANNA
          I don't think that's possible.

                    SCOTT
          What if --

                    ANNA
          What if monkeys suddenly flew out
          of your ass?

                    SCOTT
          That would be something. I wouldn't
          have to worry about painting any
          more. We'd be rich on appearance
          fees.

                    ANNA
          Did you choose to be an artist?

                    SCOTT
          No.

                    ANNA
          No. It's in your soul. It's who you
          are. You didn't have to go to
          school to be who you are, you just
          did it. Tell me again where your
          art comes from.

Scott pauses.

                    ANNA (CONT'D)
          Please, I love hearing you tell it.

Scott smiles.

                    SCOTT
          I close my eyes. I don't see
          darkness. I see an image. As it
          forms, sometimes it's defined and
          clear; definitive. Other times it's
          soft-focused, as if in the
          distance, obscured by atmosphere.

Scott closes his eyes and Anna watches. She looks at him
adoringly.

                    SCOTT (CONT'D)
          On the rare occasion it's only in
          my peripheral vision. Those are the
          most maddening. They're there but I
          cannot clearly make them out. I do
          my best to immediately capture the
          image in my sketchbook, then later
          realize it on a canvas or paper.

Scott opens his eyes to see Anna staring, lovingly at him.

She places her hand on his arm.

                    ANNA
          And why to you paint?

                    SCOTT
          I guess it's that inner desire to
          express myself. We all have that.

                    ANNA
          Sure, just some of us are more
          equipped to do it well for public
          consumption. You have that.

                    SCOTT
          So do you.

                    ANNA
          Not in the same way. I'm able to be
          creative for my clients in how I
          tell their story in a press release
          or how I arrange an event. I love
          what I do, but what you do is
          totally different. I connect with
          my clients. You are trying to
          connect with a huge audience.

                    SCOTT
          I paint simply to connect with and
          solidify the images my mind
          produces for me. Mind to hand, hand
          to canvas.

                    ANNA
          So make that connection.

INT. APARTMENT STUDIO - DAY

Scott sits in his comfy chair, a sketch pad and pen in his
hand.

He closes his eyes and concentrates.

When he opens his eyes he sketches in his book. His pen flies
over the page leaving behind marks, patterns and shapes.

Crosshatching. Shading. Bold lines. Thin lines.

Scott fills the page and then another with ink.

The more he sketches the more frantic his work becomes until
the pen is scraping the paper, ink barely releasing from the
nib.

The page rips where Scott runs the pen over it so often that
the paper is wore through.

Scott stops. Spent. Like the ink from the pen, he has emptied
himself on the page.

He looks at the results and frowns.

His phone RINGING revives him from his stupor.

Scott answers.

                    BRETT (O.C.)
          Hey, buddy. How's it going? Anna
          told me you cleaned the studio.
          Find Jimmy Hoffa's bones?

                    SCOTT
          Should I be concerned that you talk
          with Anna so much?

                    BRETT (O.C.)
          The way you look and the way she
          looks? I would be.

                    SCOTT
          What's up, Brett?

                    BRETT (O.C.)
          Just checking on my number one
          artist in the world.

                    SCOTT
          I'm fine. Putting some thoughts on
          paper.

                    BRETT (O.C.)
          Outstanding. So we're on for the
          show? I'll put it on the calendar.
          How does June sound?

                    SCOTT
          That's only four months.

                    BRETT (O.C.)
          No getting anything past you.

Scott looks at his sketch book. He closes the cover.

                    SCOTT
          That seems soon.

                    BRETT (O.C.)
          C'mon! This from the guy who turned
          out twelve pieces in two months.

                    SCOTT
          Of derivative shit, remember?

                    BRETT (O.C.)
          Not my words, man.

                    SCOTT
          I don't know, Brett. I'll call you
          when I have something.

                    BRETT (O.C.)
          Don't make me wait, buddy.

                    SCOTT
          You mean like your wife does?

> BRETT (O.C.)
> Now, that's just hurtful.

> SCOTT
> I'll call you.

> BRETT (O.C.)
> You know I love you?

> SCOTT
> Talk soon.

> BRETT (O.C.)
> Oh, leaves me --

Scott disconnects the phone.

Scott opens his sketch book again and flips through the pages.

Anna enters.

> ANNA
> Was that Brett?

> SCOTT
> Yep.

Anna walks over and sits on the arm of the chair.

> ANNA
> How's it going?

> SCOTT
> See for yourself.

Scott, hands Anna the sketchbook and leans back. Closing his eyes.

Anna flips through the pages, slowly. Deliberately.

She closes the cover.

Scott lifts his head and looks at her.

> SCOTT (CONT'D)
> So?

> ANNA
> It's a start.

Scott takes the sketchbook back and places it on the table.

                    SCOTT
          It sucks.

                    ANNA
          I didn't say that.

Scott stands. He walks away.

                    SCOTT
          I know it does.

                    ANNA
          You're just exploring ideas.

                    SCOTT
          I have no new ideas.

INT. APARTMENT - BEDROOM - NIGHT

Scott slips into the darkened bedroom. He moves silently so
as not to wake Anna.

Anna rustles under the covers. She rolls over and opens her
eyes.

Scott undresses for bed, stripping down to his underwear.

                    ANNA
          I wondered if you were ever coming
          to bed.

                    SCOTT
          I'm sorry about earlier.

                    ANNA
          I know you are. You're like a child
          who lashes out from time to time
          but doesn't really mean it.

                    SCOTT
          Great. So now I'm childish.

                    ANNA
          That's not always a bad thing.
              (beat)
          A child doesn't censor his art.
          They create for the simple pleasure
          of creating. There are no wrong
          decisions. Once you find your
          artistic child you'll be on the
          road.

Scott climbs into bed and kisses Anna on the forehead.

>   SCOTT
>   I'm sorry I woke you.
>
>   ANNA
>   It's okay. Thankfully I wasn't
>   dreaming about Chris Hemsworth, or
>   I would be really upset.
>
>   SCOTT
>   Good night.
>
>   ANNA
>   Night. I love you.
>
>   SCOTT
>   Love you.

Scott lays down. He closes his eyes.

A moment passes and he opens his eyes.

Scott slips out of bed as carefully as he can.

Anna moves.

>   ANNA
>   Find your inner child?
>
>   SCOTT
>   I'll let you know.
>   (beat)
>   This is your fault.
>
>   ANNA
>   We all suffer for your art.

INT. APARTMENT STUDIO - LATER

- MONTAGE

[IF POSSIBLE, MUSIC FROM PETER GABRIEL - "COME TALK TO ME" OR
"ONLY US"]

- Scott sits in his underwear at a desk with his sketchbook.
He works over a number of pages.

- CU of ink flowing from nib onto page.

- Scott switches from sketching to speed painting on paper.

- He applies washes of color on paper.

- He tears a page from his pad and crumbles it up. Tossing it on the floor.

- A mountain of pages sit on the floor by Scott's feet.

- Scott takes a swig from a bottle of whiskey.

- Scott paces his studio.

- Scott sits in his chair and closes his eye in a meditative stay.

- Scott paints more on his pad.

- He tacks a few pages to his wall. Then tears them down.

- Scott lights a joint and smokes it.

- He tries sketching in his pad again. Random scribbles. Anything to find his inner child.

- The pile of paper on the floor grows.

- TIME-LAPSE SERIES OF SCENES

- Scott stares at paint drying on his palette.

- Scott sits in his comfy chair and flips through magazines. Searching for inspiration.

- CU of charcoal on paper.

- CU of ink on paper.

- CU of paint squeezed from tubes.

- CU brush mixing paint on palette.

- CU brush scrubbing roughly on a canvas.

[THROUGHOUT SCOTT'S OUTFITS WILL CHANGE. TIME OF DAY WILL CHANGE. THERE WILL BE SOME REPETITION OF SCENES.

This has become Scott's routine - sketching, speed painting studies, drinking, smoking, studying, throwing things in frustration.]

- Anna watches from the doorway

FADE TO BLACK.

INT. APARTMENT - DAY

Anna, dressed in casual business attire enters the apartment.
She sets her keys on the console by the door and walks into
the living space.

Scott is passed out on the sofa. His sketchbook resting on
his chest.

Anna gently wakes him.

Scott opens his eyes, surprised to see Anna standing above
him. He wipes the drool from his chin.

>   SCOTT
>   Hey, babe. You're home early.

>   ANNA
>   Actually, you're sleeping late.

>   SCOTT
>   Really? What time is it?

>   ANNA
>   I assume you haven't started
>   dinner?

Scott works to become coherent.

>   SCOTT
>   I'm sorry. I'll whip something up
>   right now.

>   ANNA
>   Don't worry about it. I'll figure
>   something out.

>   SCOTT
>   I'm sorry.
>   (beat)
>   You want a drink?

Scott holds up the half empty bottle that sits next to him on
the couch.

>   ANNA
>   Sure. Pour me some while I change.

Anna exits to the bedroom.

INT. APARTMENT - KITCHEN - NIGHT

Anna and Scott sit in silence at the dinner table.

Each plate looks like a work of art, the way the food is prepared and presented. Anna is an artist in her own way.

                    SCOTT
          Sorry again about dinner.

                    ANNA
          It worked out.

                    SCOTT
          Sure did. Maybe I should forget
          more often.

Anna's expression says differently.

                    SCOTT (CONT'D)
          Or not.

The two eat in silence again.

                    SCOTT (CONT'D)
          Brett's coming be later this week.

                    ANNA
          That's good.

Scott sits silently.

                    ANNA (CONT'D)
          Or not.
               (beat)
          Will you have anything to show him?

                    SCOTT
          He can't expect me to have
          something so soon.

                    ANNA
          It's been --

                    SCOTT
          I know how long it's been. I'm not
          ready yet.

More silence.

                    SCOTT (CONT'D)
          What is life?

Anna puts her fork down and looks at Scott. She lifts her wine glass up for a refill.

                    ANNA
          If we're having that conversation
          then I'll take more wine.

Scott obliges and fills her glass.

                    SCOTT
          What is art?

                    ANNA
          Which answer should I pretend I
          know first?

                    SCOTT
          I think we see and perceive what we
          want to see in art -- projecting
          our own ideas and ideals onto a
          piece -- often giving it greater
          importance than the artists
          originally intended. Not all art
          has a deeper meaning, and not all
          artists have some profound
          statement to make. Sometimes a work
          is just art for art sake.

                    ANNA
          Decorative art?

                    SCOTT
          Whatever. You know as well as I do
          that term is condescending to
          artists who wish to be seen as
          collectible.

                    ANNA
          So what would you call it?

                    SCOTT
          Why does it have to be labeled? As
          viewers we need to enjoy art simply
          for the mark that is makes in
          space. Enjoying a piece for what it
          is, a beautiful work of paint on
          canvas. Nothing more.

                    ANNA
          Profound.

Scott puts his fork down and stares at Anna.

                    SCOTT
          Are you mocking me?

                    ANNA
          Not at all. I understand what
          you're saying and I don't disagree.

                    SCOTT
          But, do you agree?

                    ANNA
          The point you are trying to make is
          that abstract art is not meant to
          tell a story, but simply to
          encourage the imagination of the
          viewer.

                    SCOTT
          Yes! Exactly.

                    ANNA
          Where are you going with this?

                    SCOTT
          I don't know, but I think I've been
          so caught up in trying to find a
          message, some hidden meaning in my
          art, to make it profound for the
          critics, that it has become a
          block.

                    ANNA
          The child paints for pleasure.

                    SCOTT
          I've been trying.

                    ANNA
          When I first met you, you painted
          with such emotion. Passion. Art is
          about freedom, freedom to rebel.
          You are anything but free.

Scott sits and plays with his food.

                    SCOTT
          You know, Gorky said, "Abstraction
          allows man to see with his mind
          what he cannot see physically with
          his eyes. Abstract art enables the
          artist to perceive beyond the
          tangible, to extract the infinite
          out of the finite. It is the
          emancipation of the mind. It is an
          exploration into unknown areas."

Anna swirls the wine in her glass.

                    ANNA
          No offense but what does this
          mental masturbation have to do with
          you painting something you are
          happy with?

Scott laughs.

                    SCOTT
          You're right. You're right.

                    ANNA
          I really think you're over thinking
          all of this.

                    SCOTT
          I know. I'm becoming the very
          elitist, intellectual bullshit
          artist I promised myself I would
          never become.

INT. APARTMENT STUDIO - DAY

Scott works in his studio. He paints on a large canvas on the
easel. He seems pleased.

Anna enters.

She watches, far enough away so as not to disturb him.

                    ANNA
          Are you pleased with your progress?

Scott steps back and studies his work.

                    SCOTT
          I think I am.
               (beat)
          What do you think?

                    ANNA
          Does it matter?

                    SCOTT
          Even though I paint for myself, all
          artist seek validation for their
          work.

Anna kisses Scott.

                    ANNA
          Then I validate you, Scott Martin.

Scott smiles.

                    SCOTT
          Thanks.

Anna exits. Scott returns to painting.

INT. APARTMENT - STUDIO - DAY

Brett leafs through Scott's sketches and studies the work on
the easel.

Scott stands near him, almost crowding him.

Brett reacts to how close Scott stands next to him.

                    BRETT
          We dating all of a sudden?

                    SCOTT
          Sorry.
               (beat)
          So?

Brett studies the work more.

                    BRETT
          I'm glad to see you working.

                    SCOTT
          Not really the enthusiasm I was
          hoping for.

Brett stutters.

                    BRETT
          I have to pee.

                    SCOTT
          You know where the bathroom is.

                    BRETT
          Let me drain the vein and I'll be
          able to think straight.

Brett walks towards the door.

                    SCOTT
          That'd be a first.

Brett stops.

                    BRETT
          Funny. If this art thing doesn't
          work maybe you can be a stand-up.

INT. APARTMENT - CONTINUOUS

Brett exits the studio and enters the main living area. He
sees Anna and rushes to her.

                    ANNA
          So? What'd you think?

                    BRETT
          I think we have a problem.

                    ANNA
          Why?

                    BRETT
          I thought you used to his muse?

                    ANNA
          Used to be being the operative
          term, apparently.

                    BRETT
          What happened?

                    ANNA
          Scott seems excited about this new
          direction.

                    BRETT
          If by new direction you mean taking
          himself out of being considered a
          gallery artist, then, by all means
          keep heading down that road.

                    ANNA
          It's not that bad.

Brett gives Anna a look as if to say, "Yes, it is."

                    BRETT
          Well you need to fix this, and
          fast.

                    ANNA
          When did this become my problem?

                    BRETT
          When your man in there started
          staring at his navel instead of
          producing work I can sell.

                    ANNA
          What do you want me to do about it?
          We've talked. I've listened.

                    BRETT
          Try a blowjob. Hell, even a hand
          job might help at this point.

                    ANNA
          It's not that bad, Brett. I like
          the new style.

                    BRETT
          Great, then you can sell his work
          at the local craft bazaar because
          that's where he's heading.

Scott peaks out of the studio.

                    SCOTT
          You done, Brett.

                    BRETT
          Just about. Anna stopped me.

Anna reacts exasperated.

                    SCOTT
          Well hurry up. I want to show you
          the studies for the next three
          pieces.

                    BRETT
          Be right there.

Scott disappears into the studio.

Brett, behaving more anxious and neurotic by the second,
turns back to Anna.

                    BRETT (CONT'D)
          If his studies look like what's on
          the easel then I guarantee you
          anything I produced in the bathroom
          has a better chance of selling.

                    ANNA
          Then tell him that. He listens to
          you.

                    BRETT
          When things are good. When things
          are bad... it's better if it comes
          from you.

                    ANNA
          So I'm the bad cop?

                    BRETT
          Can you wear a sexy cop costume?

                    ANNA
          Brett!

                    BRETT
          Sorry. I get perverted when I'm
          stressed.

                    ANNA
          Do you honestly believe his new
          work is that bad?

                    BRETT
          What I just saw is so bad, it makes
          Hitler's work look like a Picasso.

Anna rolls her eyes.

                    SCOTT (O.C.)
          Brett, hurry up!

Brett reacts as jittery as a Chihuahua.

                    BRETT
          Anna, please. You have to do
          something.

                    ANNA
          I don't know what magic spell you
          think I have over him.

                    BRETT
          I don't know either but it's always
          worked before.

Anna thinks.

                    ANNA
          Scott has been talking about going
          away for a little while.

Brett reacts excitedly.

                         BRETT
               Do that!

                         SCOTT (O.C.)
               I hear you still talking. Pee and
               get back in here!

                         BRETT
                    (yelling)
               I'm going in the sink.

Anna reacts disgusted.

                         BRETT (CONT'D)
                    (whispering)
               We both want the same thing. We
               want to see Scott return to his
               glory. Maybe a vacation will help
               him.

                         ANNA
               He has been working around the
               clock to prepare for you.

                         BRETT
               It shows.

                         ANNA
               Be nice.

                         BRETT
               I am.

                         ANNA
               What about the show? If we leave
               for a week it might be too late. He
               won't have enough time to get
               everything finished.

                         BRETT
               He'll be finished if we show what
               he's working on. I can postpone the
               show. We haven't even started
               promoting it yet.

Scott enters the room again.

                         SCOTT
               Brett, did you really have to pee,
               or are you just flirting with Anna?

Brett reacts like a child caught with his hand in the cookie
jar.

                    BRETT
          Both?

                    SCOTT
          Get in here. You know Anna only
          likes men who've gone through
          puberty.

                    BRETT
          Nice.

                    SCOTT
          C'mon.

Scott walks back into the studio.

Brett turns to Anna, pleading.

                    BRETT
          Come with me.

INT. APARTMENT - STUDIO - CONTINUOUS

Anna and Brett enter the studio.

Scott has laid more color studies on his desk.

                    SCOTT
          It's a good thing I'm not a jealous
          man.

                    BRETT
               (nervously)
          Nothing to be jealous of. Anna and
          I just had a quickie on the kitchen
          counter. I would sterilize before
          you eat off it.

                    ANNA
               (disgusted)
          Brett.

                    SCOTT
          Don't worry. The amount of time you
          were together, you could have
          finished and still had time to
          clean up.

                    BRETT
          We're thinking of sneaking away for
          a vacation. Hey! You too should
          consider doing that.

Anna rolls her eyes again. Brett is in full salesman mode.

                    SCOTT
          We're planning a trip to the Hill
          Country.

                    BRETT
          Yes! A change of scenery. Fresh
          air. Clear the head.

                    SCOTT
          Now that travel plans are settled
          can we please get back to the work?

Brett pivots and schmoozes his friend and client.

                    BRETT
          I like where you're heading. It's a
          wonderful exploration.

                    SCOTT
          Come look at these studies for the
          rest of the series.

Scott is excited to show more work to Brett now that he
received some validation.

Brett saunters to the desk and looks, enthusiastically at the
work.

But, when Scott looks at him, Brett feigns excitement.

Anna watches from a distance, both physically and
emotionally.

                    BRETT
          Yep. Totally. I see where you're
          going.

Brett looks over his shoulder at Anna and grimaces.

Anna frowns.

                    SCOTT
          I'm excited.

                    BRETT
          Me too.

                    SCOTT
          I think we should move the show up
          a few weeks. I want people to see
          my new work as soon as possible.

Brett reacts shocked, surprised, dismayed.

>   BRETT
>   Actually, if you're going to go on
>   vacation, maybe we should postpone
>   for a few weeks. Give you time. Re-
>   evaluate when you return.

>   SCOTT
>   You think?

>   BRETT
>   Definitely.
>   (to Anna)
>   Right?

Scott turns to Anna.

>   ANNA
>   Makes sense.

Scott looks at Anna then Brett.

>   SCOTT
>   Okay. I'm fine with that.

Brett reacts relived.

>   SCOTT (CONT'D)
>   This calls for a celebration.

>   BRETT
>   Absolutely!

Scott opens a drawer and produces a sandwich bag of
marijuana. He holds it up and smiles.

INT. APARTMENT - LATER

Anna and Scott sit on the sofa together while Brett lies on
the floor. The room is filled with smoke. Bags of chips and
cookies are strewn on the coffee table.

Brett munches on a cookie.

>   BRETT
>   All I'm saying is, if someone wants
>   to buy a piece because it goes with
>   their sofa... fine. My commission
>   is the same.

>   ANNA
>   You're a real patron of the arts.

Brett sits up.

> BRETT
> Hold on. Don't mistake my cavalier
> attitude towards a sale as a slight
> to my appreciation for art. Scott,
> c'mon, I've supported you since
> nearly the beginning of your
> career. You know your work speaks
> to me in my bowels.

Scott hits the joint and blows out. He hands it to Anna who
takes a hit.

> SCOTT
> Not sure I wanted to know that.

> BRETT
> My point is, I feel you.

Brett reaches out as if he is touching Scott.

> BRETT (CONT'D)
> I feel this.

Brett reaches towards one of Scott's paintings hanging
nearby.

> BRETT (CONT'D)
> I can't make others feel it. But, I
> am more than happy to take their
> money if this matches Fifi's dog
> collar. You have to separate a
> gallery's commerce with your need
> for relevance and historical
> significance. Will your art hang in
> the Louvre or the Guggenheim?
> Maybe. If that what's important to
> you?

Brett waits for Scott's reaction.

Scott stares at his art.

> SCOTT
> I keep thinking about the review --

> BRETT
> Let that go, man. It doesn't
> matter.

Scott stands. Surprisingly energetic.

                    SCOTT
          You're wrong! It does mater, or
          else we wouldn't even be having
          this conversation.

                    BRETT
          We're celebrating remember? Pass
          the joint.

Anna passes the joint to Brett. Scott ignores him.

                    SCOTT
          He said I was sliding into
          decorative art.

                    BRETT
          He was full of shit --

                    SCOTT
          Was he? I mean, I haven't changed
          my style in years. I've become
          comfortable. My art doesn't have to
          have meaning but at least I was
          always exploring and experimenting.
          Now, I'm safe.

Scott paces with a manic energy. Anna and Brett try to track
with him as he moves around the room.

                    SCOTT (CONT'D)
          I don't give a shit about labels.
          Art is rebellion. How do you label
          rebellion? If someone told Johnny
          Rotten there were rules to music he
          would have flipped them the bird
          and told that to piss-off. Who
          dictates what art is? Who's to say
          if art is one thing or another?

Scott's pacing picks up speed.

                    BRETT
          Scott, man, can you maybe sit down
          and make your point? Your making me
          dizzy.
               (to Anna)
          Is he making you dizzy?

Anna, eyes glazed over, just smiles.

                    SCOTT
          I reject these notions and call
          them untrue!
                    (MORE)

                    SCOTT (CONT'D)
          I rebel against the rules that
          critics would cram down our
          throats!

                    BRETT
          Yeah, they can all piss-off!

Brett flips his middle finger in the air to no one in
particular.

                    SCOTT
          I rebel against the rules that
          would try to govern rebellion.

Brett falls onto his back and holds his fist in the air.

                    BRETT
          Power to the people!

                    SCOTT
          Art is emotion. I lost my emotion
          and settled into complacency. I
          need to shake things up.

                    BRETT
          You're certainly emotional now.
          You're the only person I know who
          becomes more active when they're
          stoned.

Scott looks at Anna.

Anna watches, bemused.

Scott continues to pace, gesturing wildly, as if punctuating
his points in the air.

[DURING SCOTT'S MONOLOGUE, CUT IN IMAGES OF PAINTINGS BY
KANDINSKY, HOFMANN, ROTHKO, AND GOTTLIED.]

                    SCOTT
          Decorative. Derivative. Modern.
          Contemporary. These are just words.
          They hold no meaning to the art.
          Did you known that the term
          abstract expressionism was meant as
          a derogatory phrase when it first
          was used to describe the work of
          Kandinsky and Hofmann? Hell even
          the term Impressionism was meant as
          a slight.
                    (MORE)

                    SCOTT (CONT'D)
          Gottlieb and Rothko, wrote a letter
          in response to their critics: "To
          us art is an adventure into an
          unknown world, which can be
          explored only by those willing to
          take the risks. This world of the
          imagination is fancy-free and
          violently opposed to common sense.
          It is our functions as artists to
          make the spectator see the world
          our way—not his way."

Brett looks around confused.

                    BRETT
          I didn't know that, buddy.
              (to Anna)
          Are you following any of this?

Anna simply smiles.

                    SCOTT
          How can a critic try to apply
          common sense to art when it is
          violently opposed to such things?
          How can it be decorative? Or, fine?
          Or, collectible? Or, any other
          label? A lamp can be decorative and
          artistic! A chair design can be
          decorative and artistic as well as
          functional. Art isn't functional.
          It serves no function other than to
          elicit emotion. Either the viewer
          has an emotion about the art or
          they don't. Whether the work goes
          well with a sofa is not the point.
          But, does it go well with your
          feelings? Does it cause you to stir
          in your soul? Or heart? Or bowels?

Scott reaches down and rubs Brett's stomach.

                    BRETT
          That's great, man.

Scott stops. Stares at Brett, then Anna.

He walks to his studio and closes the door.

Brett looks to Anna for explanation but she simply sits
smiling on the sofa.

                    BRETT (CONT'D)
          What the hell just happened?

INT. APARTMENT - MORNING

Brett folds a blanket and places it on the sofa.

He runs his hand like a comb through his hair. He has serious bed head.

Scott enters the room and closes the bedroom door behind him.

> SCOTT
> Good, you're up.

> BRETT
> Does this establishment serve breakfast?

> SCOTT
> Yep. There's a McDonald's on the corner.

> BRETT
> That's going to reflect in your Yelp rating.

Scott walks to the kitchen and opens the refrigerator. He holds up eggs.

Brett walks towards him and nods his approval.

> BRETT (CONT'D)
> Coffee?

Scott points to the Keurig.

> SCOTT
> Help yourself.

> BRETT
> So, I've been thinking --

> SCOTT
> Always a dangerous beginning to a conversation.

> BRETT
> Hear me out. We've brought in a few new artists and I think you should check out their work.

Scott breaks an egg into a bowl then discards the shell into the sink.

> BRETT (CONT'D)
> Just to see what's emerging.

                    SCOTT
          Are you seriously trying to
          motivate me by trying to have me
          look at my competition?

                    BRETT
          I didn't know art was a
          competition.

                    SCOTT
          It shouldn't be, but we all know we
          compete for a gallery director's
          attention and a collector's wallet.

                    BRETT
          I just thought you might be
          interested in the work of some up
          and comers.

Scott whips the eggs.

Scott pours the whipped eggs into the skillet where they
begin sizzling.

                    BRETT (CONT'D)
          Come down to the gallery and see
          them first hand.

Anna enters the room. Dressed nicely for the day.

                    ANNA
          Well, if this isn't a woman's
          dream, two men to wait on her hand
          and foot.

Anna takes the coffee mug from Brett's hand and begins
drinking it.

She walks over to the Scott and kisses his cheek.

Brett is flabbergasted but recovers and start the process of
making another cup of coffee.

                    SCOTT
          Sure. I'll swing by when I can.

                    BRETT
          Great.

                    ANNA
          Swing by where?

                          SCOTT
          Brett is trying inspire me by
          looking at his new artists.

Anna frowns at Brett.

                          BRETT
          What? It was just an idea.

                          ANNA
          Let us take our vacation and then
          we can talk art again.

INT. BEDROOM - NIGHT

SERIES OF SHOTS

Stylized extreme CU (NO NUDITY)

- The caress of a hand on the curve of a back.

- The flow of paint from the brush to the canvas.

- A kiss on the nape of the neck.

- A dab of paint.

- The sucking of a finger.

- A brush mixes paint on a palette.

- Fingers entwines in hair.

- Short strokes of a brush.

- A mouth open in desire.

- A long stroke of a brush in circular motion.

- A passionate kiss.

- A brush dipped in a jar of water and swirled.

INT. APARTMENT - DAY

The apartment door opens. Anna and Scott enter. Scott carries
and pulls a number of suitcases.

                          ANNA
          I told you I would help.

                    SCOTT
          What kind of gentleman would make a
          woman lift a finger?

Scott drops one of the bags and the others tumble with it.

The two laugh.

                    ANNA
          While I appreciate the chivalry, I
          also want to make sure it all gets
          home in one piece.

                    SCOTT
          You afraid I broke that slinky
          negligee?

Scott scoops Anna off her feet and twirls her.

                    ANNA
          We might need to go on holiday more
          often.

                    SCOTT
          That's what I'm saying!

Scott puts Anna down and she picks up one of her bags.

                    ANNA
          I'll start unpacking.

                    SCOTT
          Seems fair since I did all the
          heavy lifting.

                    ANNA
          Whatever. You packed one pair of
          shorts and T-shirt.

                    SCOTT
          All I needed... wasn't it.

The two giggle like newlyweds on their honeymoon.

                    ANNA
          You going into your studio?

                    SCOTT
          Nah.
              (beat)
          Want me to help you unpack? I can
          help you look for that negligee.

Scott teases Anna.

Anna deflects.

                    ANNA
          You're obviously feeling rested. I
          figured you'd be anxious to get
          back to work.

                    SCOTT
          That's just it. It's work. I don't
          want to spoil this good mood.

                    ANNA
          Brett's expecting --

Scott's mood shifts.

                    SCOTT
          I don't want to discuss Brett or
          the show.

Scott walks away.

He flops down on the sofa.

Anna puts the bag down. She joins Scott on the sofa.

                    ANNA
          Want to tell me what's going on?

                    SCOTT
          I'd rather continue what we started
          in Fredericksburg.

Scott nuzzles Anna. She plays along but gently stops Scott
after a moment.

                    ANNA
          It's not like you to decline time
          in the studio. What's going on?

                    SCOTT
          I'm not feeling it.

                    ANNA
          I assume you're talking about your
          art, cause you felt everything you
          could this weekend.

Scott smiles.

                    SCOTT
          This weekend was exactly what I...
          What we needed.

                    ANNA
          It was fun.

                    SCOTT
          It was more than that. It was life
          changing.

                    ANNA
          Well, I knew I was good but not
          that good.

Scott laughs.

                    SCOTT
          You are good, but do you realize
          that was the first time I've taken
          any time off from painting in
          years? It was refreshing to not
          have to be producing. To have to
          create. To perform.

                    ANNA
          I didn't realize you felt that way.

                    SCOTT
          I didn't either until I didn't have
          to. It's like that Lennon song,
          where he sings about just sitting
          and watching the wheels go round
          and round. He was carefree.
          Unburden. That's how I want to
          live.

                    ANNA
          Okay.

                    SCOTT
          I'm serious. No more critics. No
          more shows. No more pressure to be
          creative.

Anna sits back to consider this.

                    ANNA
          Can we afford to do this?

                    SCOTT
          You make enough and we have the
          savings.

                    ANNA
          Sure. What about you?

                    SCOTT
          What do you mean?

                    ANNA
          Can you afford not to create? You
          know the mood you get in if you
          haven't been productive.

Scott thinks.

                    SCOTT
          It's worth a try. The other way
          isn't working.

                    ANNA
          Well, let's give it a shot. See how
          long you can last.

Scott leans towards Anna and snuggles.

                    SCOTT
          Oh, I think you know how long I can
          last.

INT. APARTMENT - BEDROOM - EVENING

Suitcases sit on the bed. Anna unpacks them.

Her phone rings. She answers.

                    ANNA
          Hey, Brett.

                    BRETT (O.C.)
          How's my favorite couple doing?

                    ANNA
          Fine. You looking for Scott?

                    BRETT (O.C.)
          Actually, I wanted to talk with you
          first.

                    ANNA
          What's up?

                    BRETT (O.C.)
          How's our boy? His head back on
          straight.

                    ANNA
          You should talk to Scott.

                    BRETT (O.C.)
          Shit. What's it going to take --

                    ANNA
          Time, Brett. Time. He's working
          through things.

                    BRETT (O.C.)
          Is he working, though? Last I saw
          you both, he was high as a kite and
          manic as fuck dancing on the edge
          of sanity.

                    ANNA
          Not much has changed, but he's more
          relaxed after having spent nearly
          seventy-two hours locked in a room
          with me.

                    BRETT (O.C.)
          Nice. I want video.

                    ANNA
          Not going to happen.

                    BRETT (O.C.)
          A guy can ask.

                    ANNA
          I'm sure your wife would appreciate
          it.

                    BRETT (O.C.)
          She'll appreciate my fat commission
          check once Scott gets his groove
          back -- I don't mean sexually --
          and his show kills.

                    ANNA
          You need talk to Scott.

Scott enters the room. Realizes Anna is on the phone with
Brett and turns to leave.

Anna SNAPS her fingers.

Scott pivots and turns back to face her.

Anna motions for Scott to take the phone. Scott shakes his
head, NO.

Anna quietly stomps her foot. Frustrated.

                    BRETT (O.C.)
          How concerned should I be?

                    ANNA
          I don't know. Call him.

Scott rolls his eyes. Now he is frustrated.

Anna smiles devilishly.

                    BRETT (O.C.)
          I don't want to disturb him if he's
          working.

                    ANNA
          But it's okay to disturb me?

                    BRETT (O.C.)
          C'mon, Anna, we're a team. We work
          together to keep our boy sane.

                    ANNA
          Well, so far this team has
          consisted of me, so do your part.
          I've got to go, Brett.

                    BRETT (O.C.)
          Wait, don't hang up --

Anna hangs up.

                    SCOTT
          Brett?

                    ANNA
          You should call him.

                    SCOTT
          I don't have anything to tell him.

                    ANNA
          Tell him that.

                    SCOTT
          That'll go over well.

                    ANNA
          He's your friend. He'll understand.

                    SCOTT
          He's also my director who counts on
          me for his own living.

                    ANNA
               Call him.

Anna tosses her phone at Scott.

INT. APARTMENT - DAY

Anna walks through the apartment looking for Scott.

INT. APARTMENT - STUDIO - CONTINUOUS

She enters the studio and finds Scott sitting and reading a
book by Kandinksky. A stack of books about Rothko, Pollock,
Scully and others sit on the table near his feet.

                    ANNA
               Hey.

                    SCOTT
               Hey.

Anna walks over and sits near Scott.

                    ANNA
               You ever call Brett?

                    SCOTT
               Nope.

Scott continues to read. Anna watches. Waits.

                    ANNA
               You going to?

                    SCOTT
               Not right now.

                    ANNA
               But later?

Scott puts the book down. He shows his frustration for being
disturbed.

                    SCOTT
               I thought we agreed I wasn't going
               to paint any longer?

                    ANNA
               We did. I just thought it would be
               wise to let Brett know that
               considering he's planning a solo
               show for you in a few weeks.

Scott returns to reading his book.

                    SCOTT
          Not really my concern.

Anna bends the book down so she looks Scott in the face.

                    ANNA
          I'm cool with you quitting. I am.
          But being a dick to your best
          friend. I'm not fine with that.

Scott puts the book down and faces Anna.

                    ANNA (CONT'D)
          You want to tell me what's really
          going on?

                    SCOTT
          I'm afraid.

Anna's mood shifts.

                    ANNA
          What do you have to be afraid of?

                    SCOTT
          What if the critics are right?

                    ANNA
          Are you seriously still concerned
          about this?

                    SCOTT
          I guess I let the criticism affect
          me more than I care to admit.

                    ANNA
          Okay. So let's work through this.
          What's the worst that can happen?

                    SCOTT
          I think every creative person at
          one time or another fears that one
          day we're going to be exposed as a
          fraud.

                    ANNA
          Honey, you're career has spanned
          nearly two decades. I think, if you
          were going to be found out, it
          would have happened a long time
          ago.

                    SCOTT
               (sarcastically)
          Thanks.

                    ANNA
          You know I'm kidding. But, you have
          to be too.

                    SCOTT
          I don't know. Honestly, I'm so
          wrapped up in my head that I don't
          see like I used to.

                    ANNA
          You mean when you close your eyes?

                    SCOTT
          Yeah. For the first time, I do see
          darkness.

Anna comforts Scott.

                    SCOTT (CONT'D)
          And then...

                    ANNA
          Yeah?

                    SCOTT
          What if you don't want to be with a
          burned out old coot.

                    ANNA
          You forgot, moody.

                    SCOTT
          I'm serious.

                    ANNA
          But I love my burned out, moody,
          old coot.
               (beat)
          Scott, I'm not in love with you
          because of your art. Neither one of
          us are that shallow. I would love
          you even if you were a window
          washer.

                    SCOTT
          That's good because I'm applying
          next week.

>   ANNA
> Passion. That's what the critics
> say is missing from your work.
> That's all you need to have
> rekindled in your spirit. You
> certainly have it in the bedroom...
> now put that on the canvas.

>   SCOTT
> If I put what we did this weekend
> on canvas, Brett won't be able to
> show it in his gallery.

>   ANNA
> Good. You're the rebel, remember?
> Show me the rebellion.

INT. APARTMENT - DAY

Anna sits at the kitchen table typing on her laptop. Her cell
phone is near her and she speaks to a co-worker on SPEAKER
PHONE.

>   ANNA
> I'm sending you the itinerary for
> the weekend's events.

>   CO-WORKING (O.C.)
> Sounds good. Did you receive the
> draft of the press release?

Anna clicks a few buttons.

>   ANNA
> Yes. I haven't read it yet, but I
> will.

Scott enters the room from the studio. He waves a book about
Rothko in the air. His energy is palatable. His stride
confident.

>   SCOTT
> Rothko was a genius!

>   ANNA
> Let me call you back.

Anna disconnects the phone.

Scott sits down at the table and places the book in front of
Anna, then stands again. His energy will not allow him to sit
still.

                    SCOTT
          You've got to read this.

                    ANNA
                (frustrated)
          I'm kind of in the middle of --

                    SCOTT
          Fine. I'll just give you the
          highlights.

Anna closes her laptop.

                    ANNA
          Okay.

Scott paces around the table making it impossible for Anna to
keep eye contact with him. She attempts to for the first two
laps, then simply stares at the book, flipping through the
pages.

[CUT IN IMAGES OF PAINTINGS BY ROTHKO.]

                    SCOTT
          Rothko resisted any attempts to
          interpret his paintings. He once
          said, "No possible set of notes can
          explain our" meaning his generation
          of American abstract artists,
          "paintings. Their explanation must
          come out of a consummated
          experience between picture and
          onlooker. The appreciation of art
          is a true marriage of minds."

Anna stares at Scott.

                    ANNA
          That's just great.

                    SCOTT
          He also said, "The fact that one
          usually begins with drawing is
          already academic. We," again
          referring to the abstract artist of
          the time, "start with color."
          That's it!

Anna can only stare.

                    SCOTT (CONT'D)
          Don't you get it?

                    ANNA
          Let's assume I don't.

[CUT IN IMAGES OF PAINTINGS BY KANDINSKY AND KELLY.]

                    SCOTT
          Kandinksy said of his work, it is
          "A departure of art from the
          objective world, and the discovery
          of a new subject matter based on an
          artist's inner need." Ellsworth
          Kelly said of Rothko's work, "What
          I like about Rothko was that there
          was no real sort of idea in the
          paintings. They were a presence,
          just pure abstraction." Then Rothko
          said, "A painting is not about
          experience. It is an experience"!
          Which is amazing because he was
          also adamant that there was no such
          thing as art for art sake!

Scott slams his palms on the table.

Anna is stunned.

                    SCOTT (CONT'D)
          So?

Anna regains her composure.

                    ANNA
          I'm glad to see your passion for
          art.

Scott waves the book in his hand.

                    SCOTT
          I've been reading Rothko and
          Kandinsky. Kandinsky talks about
          color and form in his book, those
          are the two most basic tenants of a
          painting. He says that form can
          stand alone but color cannot, it
          always has boundaries and shape of
          some kind. But color also has
          spiritual value.

                    ANNA
          It's all very interesting. I
          understand what they are saying
          about their work but what does this
          have to do with yours?

                    SCOTT
          If I'm going to paint again, then I
          have to return to the most basic
          and simplest form of art.

                    ANNA
          Haven't I been saying that all
          along?

                    SCOTT
          Yes! That's why I need you so much.
          And, it's why my art is so entwined
          with our relationship. When things
          are good between us, so is my art.

                    ANNA
          But things are great between us and
          you don't want to paint?

                    SCOTT
          I know.

                    ANNA
          I'm confused.

                    SCOTT
          I've gotten so anxious about
          critics and rules and academics. I
          have to remove everything, from my
          palette, and all rules and reason.

                    ANNA
          I'm starting to sense the last
          part.

Scott smirks at Anna.

                    SCOTT
          Stay with me.

                    ANNA
          I'm trying. Maybe we should call
          Brett.

Scott tries to sit again, then stands and paces.

                    SCOTT
          Sure. Put him on speaker.

Anna dials Brett. The line connects after two rings.

                    BRETT (O.C.)
          Hey!

                        ANNA
          Brett, you're on speaker. Scott has
          some ideas he wants to share.

Anna looks at Scott.

                        BRETT
          I'm all ears. What's up?

Anna motions for Scott to continue his rant.

                        SCOTT
          Brett. I may have figured it out.

                        BRETT
          That's great news. What are we
          figuring out?

                        SCOTT
          I need to create art that is above
          and beyond criticism.

                        BRETT (O.C.)
          We'd all love to do that, my friend
          --

                        SCOTT
          I talk. You listen.

There is silence. Then.

                        BRETT (O.C.)
               (softly)
          Okay.

                        SCOTT
          The purest form of art is
          childlike, right? Rothko called it
          primitive.

Silence.

                        BRETT (O.C.)
          Can I talk now?

                        SCOTT
          No! Listen.
               (beat)
          Even more basic is a total lack of
          substance and color.

                        BRETT (O.C.)
          I'm--

[CUT IN IMAGES OF PAINTINGS BY GUSTON AND MONDRIAN.]

                    SCOTT
          Shhhh! I need to create art that
          can not be criticized because there
          is simply nothing to critique.
          Sometimes art is simply an
          exploration into the creation of
          said art. For example, Philip
          Guston's forms consisting of thick
          vertical and horizontal brush
          strokes often canceling each other,
          and growing denser towards the
          center of the canvas. Or,
          Mondrian's plus-minus works. It's
          the very act of painting which the
          artist explores which is the focus.
          Thus the application of the paint
          is as much the art as the finished
          painting.

                    BRETT (O.C.)
          Are you talking about performance
          art?

                    SCOTT
          No, aren't you listening?

                    BRETT (O.C.)
          I thought I was but apparently not
          very well.

                    ANNA
          Explain it to us again.

                    SCOTT
          Guston said, "The painting process
          is a dialog with the picture." It
          is gestural painting if you must
          put a label on it but that is
          precisely what I am trying to
          avoid: all labels, rules,
          preconceived notions and
          perceptions. Critics feed on that
          like flies over a corpse. The
          world, society, is too full of
          these things. We need simplicity. A
          return to child-like innocence. A
          return to the primitive. The act of
          making the art is as much of the
          art as the finished result and you,
          the viewer, are able to discern
          this through viewing the final
          piece.

Anna watches Scott continue to walk round and round the table.

[CUT IN IMAGES OF PAINTINGS BY STILL.]

                SCOTT (CONT'D)
Clyfford Still rejected any
intellectualization of art and that
is exactly what the critics have
done to me. They're trying to
intellectualize something that they
shouldn't. So I'm going to create
art that cannot be
intellectualized. I will destroy
any personality of style and focus
on pure artistry. But, there in
lies the rub. How does one do that?
The very fact that I am discussing
this with you now is
intellectualize the very thing I am
attempting to do without
intellectualization. You see my
dilemma? I have to lose color.
Color can exercise enormous
influence over the physical body
and mental psyche. Is it color
versus form, or color as form?
    (beat)
Compound this with the fact that I
have always believed in art for art
sake. The purity of the mark. But
Rothko was extremely critical of
this line of thought. So where does
that leave me? I consider Rothko
and artistic deity, but he in fact
would despise my process and my way
of thinking.
    (beat)
And this is more than just about
art, this is about life as we know
it. It's about materialism and
spiritualism. Can art be both? Does
one cancel out the other? Does it
have to be this way? And by asking
these questions have we not just
come full circle again into
intellectualism? This is what I am
dealing with Droll. This is the
hurdle I must leap and it is taking
time. You can't expect it to happen
overnight. It simply can't it is
too big a problem to solve. But, I
am set on solving it.
    (MORE)

                    SCOTT (CONT'D)
          To create the most basic of art,
          and art that is above reproach
          because it is not art. It is
          nothing.

Scott pauses.

Anna sits silently. Expectantly waiting for another outburst.

There is a long silence.

                    BRETT (O.C.)
          Great! I'm convinced. So when do we
          see something?

Scott shakes his head.

                    SCOTT
          I'm afraid you may never truly see
          what I'm talking about.

                    BRETT (O.C.)
          That pains me deeply, man.

                    SCOTT
          What pains me my friend is that I
          want you to see, but until you can
          shed the business of art you will
          not truly be able to understand
          art.

Scott walks out of the room, returning to his studio.

Anna picks up the phone.

                    ANNA
          He left the room, Brett. It's just
          me.

                    BRETT (O.C.)
          What the hell was that? Did you
          break him?

                    ANNA
          I'm not sure what's going on.

                    BRETT (O.C.)
          I have an idea. You sexually
          overdosed him. That's what you did.
          You used your sexual charms for an
          entire weekend and enchanted him
          into a stupor. That's not the way a
          muse should work.

INT. APARTMENT - DAY

Anna folds laundry.

Scott moves an easel into the living room.

> ANNA
> What are you doing?

> SCOTT
> I thought it would be nice to be
> near you. You inspire me.

Anna smiles and continues to fold clothes.

Scott exits to his studio and returns with a cart of his
paints.

SERIES OF SCENES

[IF POSSIBLE PETER GABRIEL'S "STEAM"]

We never see the results of Scott's work. Many shots he is
out of focus in background.

The canvas Scott works on is large. When he paints it is like
dancing.

Scott and the canvas are backlit so his shadow shows through
the back side of the canvas.

- Scott has manic energy.

- He squirts huge amounts of paint on a glass palette.

- He scrubs his brush into the paint on the palette.

- He scrubs the brush on the canvas.

- Anna makes tea for both of them. She is careful and
deliberate, like a Japanese tea ceremony. An art onto itself.

- Scott moves from edge to edge of the canvas.

- Anna places a mug of tea near Scott. He mistakenly puts his
brush in it. Anna rolls her eyes. She smiles and removes the
mug. Scott uses the tea stained brush on the canvas.

  ECU of paint on canvas.

- Anna folds laundry. Scott in background working.

- Scott's washes his brush. Water drips everywhere.

- Anna watches the mess Scott makes.

- Scott rubs paint from his hand onto his clothes. Paint is on his clothes, in his hair, on his face.

- Anna sits at the kitchen table reading e-mail on her laptop. Scott in the background painting.

- Scott paints around the CAMERA as if it is the canvas. HE STEPS OUT OF FRAME ONCE then returns to center, studying his work.

- Anna places a new mug of tea by Scott but stops him before he can make the same mistake again.

- Anna sits watching Scott as she sips tea.

INT. APARTMENT - KITCHEN - NIGHT

Anna prepares dinner. LOUD BANGING noise can be heard in the background.

The DOORBELL RINGS.

Anna answers the door. Brett enters.

They hug.

MORE BANGING. A SHOUT.

                    SCOTT (O.C.)
          Shit!

Brett looks at Anna.

                    BRETT
          What they hell? I thought
          everything was better?

Anna shrugs and returns to the kitchen and the food preparations.

                    ANNA
          I thought so too. He's volatile --

                    BRETT
          You think?

Brett, slumps his shoulders. Defeated.

                    ANNA
          One minute he thinks he's captured
          lightning, the next...

Anna points in the direction of the studio.

A LOUD CRASH.

>   SCOTT (O.C.)
>   Piece of shit!

>   BRETT
>   How long has this been going on?

Anna nonchalantly looks at the clock on the oven.

>   ANNA
>   Half an hour.

>   BRETT
>   How long before he runs out of
>   steam?

>   ANNA
>   He should be close.

>   BRETT
>   Damnit. I thought he'd made a
>   breakthrough?

>   ANNA
>   We all did. He's been at it all
>   day.

>   BRETT
>   So what happened?

>   ANNA
>   You'll have to ask him. I thought
>   it looked great.

Brett looks towards to studio, the source of all the SHOUTING AND LOUD NOISE.

>   BRETT
>   I don't think I should interrupt
>   him.

>   ANNA
>   Wimp.

Brett looks at Anna for some support, which she isn't giving.

>   BRETT
>   I've never seen him like this.

                    ANNA
          He's second guessing everything he
          does now.

                    BRETT
          That's not good.

SLAM.

                    BRETT (CONT'D)
          Maybe I should come back?

Brett turns to leave.

Scott enters.

                    SCOTT
          Brett, when did you get here?

Brett turns around. He reacts like a deer in headlights.

                    BRETT
          Uh. I.

Brett looks to Anna for help.

                    ANNA
          He just got here.

                    SCOTT
          I thought Anna might have called
          you and told you not to come.

                    BRETT
          I can come back?

                    SCOTT
          Yeah --

                    ANNA
          No. Show him what you've been
          working on.

Scott glares at Anna. Brett does too.

                    SCOTT
          It's not ready.

                    BRETT
          Yeah. I feel I should just come
          back.

                              ANNA
                    You're here.
                         (to Scott)
                    You need to calm down. Show him.

Scott and Brett react like kids scolded by their mother.

                              SCOTT
                    Come on.

Scott retreats to his studio.

Brett looks at Anna like a young pup. Anna points a knife at
him and motions towards the studio. Slowly he moves. He looks
back to see if she means it. She keeps pointing.

INT. APARTMENT - STUDIO - CONTINUOUS

The studio has been in better shape. The easel is knocked
over. A torn canvas leans against a wall. Paint tubes are
strewn on the floor.

                              BRETT
                    New decorator?

Scott pours two glasses of whiskey.

He walks to Brett and hands him one.

Scott walks to his comfy chair and plops down into it. He
picks up a book and begins reading as he drinks his entire
glass in one gulp.

                              BRETT (CONT'D)
                    So...?

                              SCOTT
                    I've got nothing to show you.

                              BRETT
                    Anna said you've been working all
                    day and it looked good.

                              SCOTT
                    We'll have to cancel the show.

Brett reacts shocked and anger.

                              BRETT
                    We can't, Scott. I've postponed
                    once --

66.

                    SCOTT
          You have to do it again.

Brett gulps his whiskey and places the empty glass on a
table.

                    BRETT
          Easier said then done, buddy. We've
          already printed postcards and
          started promoting it on social
          media.

                    SCOTT
          Sucks for you.

                    BRETT
          Sucks for both of us. The owner
          wants this show. She's not going to
          be pleased if we pull the plug.
                    (beat)
          What happened man? The other day
          you were all excited like you had
          discovered the meaning of life.

                    SCOTT
          I did.

Scott motions around the room.

                    BRETT
          So it's a deconstructionist vibe?

Scott frowns at Brett.

                    BRETT (CONT'D)
          What do you want me to tell my
          boss?

                    SCOTT
          I don't care. Tell her whatever you
          want. Tell her I'm done.

Brett walks over and sits near Scott.

                    BRETT
          Man. I know you're going through a
          rough patch --

                    SCOTT
          Does this look like a rough patch?
          This looks like a head-on
          collision.

                    BRETT
          Tomato. Tomato. Point is, you keep
          going. You don't stop. Does a pig
          wallow in its own shit?
               (beat)
          Yeah, terrible example. Forget
          that. This too shall pass. You
          think Picasso didn't have dry
          spells? He did. But he rallied. And
          he came out on top, and so will
          you. We just have to find your
          muse.

                    SCOTT
          Picasso had many muses.

Brett stutters at his poor choice of wording.

                    BRETT
          Okay, I didn't mean like that.
          C'mon, don't mess around. Anna's
          the best thing you've got.
               (beat)
          Seriously, this show has to take
          place, man. Let me look at what you
          did.

Scott points at the canvas leaning awkwardly against the wall
with a hole in it.

Brett grimaces. He walks to the painting and lifts it from
the wall so he can see it.

                    BRETT (CONT'D)
          Honestly, brother. I like it. No. I
          love it.

Brett looks at Scott.

                    BRETT (CONT'D)
          I wouldn't screw with you. It's got
          a Lucio Fontana thing going.

Brett tries to hold the flaps of the torn canvas.

Scott sits staring.

                    SCOTT
          It's shit.

Brett lets the canvas rest against the wall again. He returns
and sits across from Scott.

                         BRETT
               Don't quit on me now, man. How long
               have you and I been friends?

Scott sits silently.

                         SCOTT
               A while.

                         BRETT
               Try nearly twenty years, brother.
               We've been through too much and
               come too far.
                         (beat)
               Can I be honest with you? I'm going
               to be honest with you. When I
               started at the gallery and I saw
               your work, I knew I wanted to be
               involved with art. I wanted to be
               involved with you. I had offers at
               hedge funds but I gave up the rich
               life to be with you.

Scott looks at Brett with a blank look on his face.

                         BRETT (CONT'D)
               It could have happened.

Brett waves that thought away like a pesky fly.

                         SCOTT
               Why do you care? You have other
               artists that are selling.

                         BRETT
               Yeah, but none I consider a true
               friend, and none that I care about
               like a brother.

Brett stands. He smiles. Puts on a good face.

                         BRETT (CONT'D)
               I'm excited. You should be. You're
               moving in the right direction, man.
               But ease off the interior
               decorating. Focus on the art.

Brett pats Scott on the knee and exits.

Scott never moves.

INT. APARTMENT - KITCHEN - CONTINUOUS

Brett exits the studio and walks to Anna in the kitchen.

              ANNA
So what'd you think?

              BRETT
I didn't hate it.

              ANNA
That's good.

              BRETT
We've... You've got to keep him on
track. He's moving in a good
direction and we... you've got to
make sure he keeps going.

              ANNA
Nice to know <u>we're</u> a team.

              BRETT
Trust me, I'm doing my part for
him. The owner asks me every day to
see something and I keep putting
her off. I won't be able to do that
for much longer. I need at least
one piece to show her, and soon.

              ANNA
I'm doing what I can, Brett.

              BRETT
I know you are and you're doing
great. You and my wife put up with
so much dealing with us than I care
to think.

              ANNA
At least you recognize that we put
up with you. That's a start.

Brett smiles sarcastically.

INT. APARTMENT - STUDIO - NIGHT

Anna enters the studio.

Scott sits in his chair with a book.

The studio is still in shambles.

Anna walks and sits on the arm of the chair.

She takes the glass of whiskey out of Scott's hand and
finishes it.

He looks at her surprised.

>   ANNA
>   You don't need this.

>   SCOTT
>   Yeah. I'm done.

>   ANNA
>   Good. You want to go to bed?

>   SCOTT
>   I'm done.

>   ANNA
>   Yep. Let's sleep it off.

>   SCOTT
>   No. I'm done.

Anna looks at Scott lovingly.

>   ANNA
>   I understand.

Scott looks up at Anna with bloodshot eyes.

>   SCOTT
>   Do you? Do you understand what it
>   feels like to know what it is you
>   want to do but have no way of doing
>   it? It's like seeing a port from
>   sea and not knowing how to land.
>   It's just right there...

Scott reaches out into thin air as if reaching for something.

>   ANNA
>   Let's go to bed. Things will look
>   better in the morning.

Anna reaches for Scott's hand.

>   SCOTT
>   You can't say that. You don't know.
>   Don't make promises you can't keep.

Anna stands. Her frustration growing.

                  ANNA
I'm not going to watch you destroy
yourself.

                  SCOTT
I know. I told you I'm done.

Anna let's this sink in. Scott looks up at her.

                  SCOTT (CONT'D)
This isn't working.

                  ANNA
Then stop trying.

                  SCOTT
This isn't working.

Scott motions between he and Anna.

                  SCOTT (CONT'D)
This.

                  ANNA
Your drunk.

                  SCOTT
That's true. The alcohol is
working.

Anna turns to leave.

                  SCOTT (CONT'D)
We've run our course. Everything
has run it's course. For everything
there is a season...

Anna turns back to face Scott.

                  ANNA
That is such bullshit.

                  SCOTT
No, it's true. It's in the bible.

Anna walks back to face off with Scott.

                  ANNA
You want to curl up and die because
you got a few shitty reviews? Fine.
I'm fine with you quitting painting
too.
                  (MORE)

                    ANNA (CONT'D)
          I'm not fine with you saying this
          is over just because you can't
          figure out what the hell you want
          to say, or do, with your art. But,
          if you're so wrapped up in this to
          think one has something to do with
          the other, well listen, I'm not
          fine with it, but I will deal with
          it, and a hell of a lot better than
          you're dealing with it.

                    SCOTT
          See, this is why is isn't working
          any longer.

                    ANNA
          Why, because I'm not putting up
          with your bullshit? You don't like
          it when I stand up for what's true?

Scott attempts to stand. He wobbles to the bar cart.

Anna reaches the cart first. She grabs the bottle of whiskey,
unscrews the cap and pours the remaining liquid on a canvas
on the floor.

                    ANNA (CONT'D)
          Look Scott. I just made art!

Anna places the empty bottle on the cart then turns and walks
away.

Before reaching the door she turns back.

                    ANNA (CONT'D)
          You want to claim this is my fault?
          I'll accept that blame because I
          love you and that's what you need
          to hear I guess. Maybe that makes
          me an enabler. Shit, I don't know
          what role I play here anymore, but
          to be honest with you Scott, it's
          not a muse you need, it's a
          counselor.

Anna exits the studio.

Scott wobbles.

INT. APARTMENT - EARLY MORNING

Scott enters the apartment followed by CHRISTY (early 30s),
the type of girl who has no problem going home with someone
after last call.

The two are obviously drunk. They stumble into the room,
giggling and trying, unsuccessfully, to be quiet.

Scott leads her to the sofa and pushes her onto it. Christy
flops down and rolls off the sofa.

The two laugh and Scott SHUSHES Christy.

Scott stumbles towards the bar cart. As if they need more to
drink.

                    CHRISTY
          I want to see your art. Show me
          your art.

                    SCOTT
          I'll show you my art.

Scott attempts to be sexy but fails spectacularly.

                    CHRISTY
          C'mon. That's why I came here.

                    SCOTT
          Oh really, that's the only reason
          you came here?

                    CHRISTY
          Well...

Christy does better at acting shy and sexy.

Scott reaches out to help Christy off the floor.

                    SCOTT
          Okay, c'mon.

It takes some effort but Scott helps Christy to her feet and
he guides her, hand around her waist, into his studio.

INT. APARTMENT - STUDIO - CONTINUOUS

The studio is completely clean and organized. Easel upright.
Canvases stacked.

Scott reacts shocked and surprised.

Christy pushes passed him into the studio.

>   CHRISTY
>   This is so cool! A real artist's
>   studio.

Scott SHUSHES her.

Christy GIGGLES and walks over to an easel.

>   CHRISTY (CONT'D)
>   So this is where you paint?

>   SCOTT
>   I used too.

>   CHRISTY
>   Paint me something.

>   SCOTT
>   I don't take requests.

Christy unbuttons a top button on her blouse.

>   CHRISTY
>   I'll make it worth your while...

>   ANNA
>   Yeah, Scott. Paint her something
>   that will impress her.

Scott spins to find Anna standing in the doorway. The
momentum from the spin causes him to fall over.

Christy re-buttons her blouse.

Anna is calm and collected. She walks over to Christy.

>   ANNA (CONT'D)
>   Hello, I'm Anna. You must be my
>   replacement.

>   CHRISTY
>   I... um... no... I didn't --

>   ANNA
>   He didn't tell you he was living
>   with someone?

Anna turns to look at Scott.

>   ANNA (CONT'D)
>   What's it been now, Scott, nearly
>   ten years, I think.
>   (MORE)

                    ANNA (CONT'D)
              (to Christy)
          In some states that's considered
          common-law marriage.

                    CHRISTY
          I'm sorry, I didn't know.

Scott lies on the floor, rubbing his face.

                    ANNA
          That's okay. I'm sure he failed to
          tell you a lot of things. You mind
          if I fill you in on a few items
          you'll need to know?

Christy looks at Scott and back to Anna. Confusion written
all over her face. What has she gotten herself into?

                    ANNA (CONT'D)
          You see, being with an artist is
          not like dating any other guy. You
          think women have mood swings when
          they have their period? It's
          nothing compared to an artist. So,
          first thing is you have to learn to
          temper the bad moods and blunt the
          ones where you think everything is
          going well but he's really just
          manic. You getting this?

Christy nods but she looks like a deer caught in headlights.

                    ANNA (CONT'D)
          Good. Next, you have to accept that
          the bad times are your fault but
          the good times are his artistic
          genius. If you can handle that,
          that's half the battle right there.
          What am I forgetting? Oh yeah, his
          ego.
              (mockingly)
          OMG. You have not experienced ego
          until you spent some time with an
          artist. I mean, who in their right
          mind would consider that if they
          splash some paint on a canvas that
          others should be amazed at it and
          pay them money for it? Does that
          sound like rational thought to you?

Christy shakes her head. She is shell-shocked. She looks for
a way out of this situation.

Scott remains seated on the floor, watching, listening.

                    ANNA (CONT'D)
          So if all of this sounds like the
          glamorous life of being an artist's
          girlfriend, he's all yours. Sure
          there are gallery openings and
          receptions where you get to dress
          in fancy clothes, sip the champagne
          and be treated like royalty, but
          those moments are few and far
          between compared to the rest.
                    (beat)
          But, if I'm being fair, loving an
          artist is also one of the most
          passionate love affairs you will
          ever experience.

Anna looks at Scott and he looks back at her.

                    ANNA (CONT'D)
          An artist is all about passion.
          Emotion. That can be scary at
          times. Everything is right there on
          the canvas. Exposed. It's honest
          and often brutal. And, there are
          moments, the best moments, of soft,
          tender affection.

Anna holds back her tears.

Scott looks away.

                    ANNA (CONT'D)
          Anyway, I just thought I'd let you
          know what you were signing up for.
          You mind if I pack my things in the
          morning?

                    CHRISTY
          Listen, I'm sorry. He didn't say
          anything about living with someone.

Both women look at Scott who tries to turn invisible.

                    CHRISTY (CONT'D)
          I'm really sorry. I wouldn't have
          come -- I don't want to get in the
          middle of anything.

                    ANNA
          My time here is done so, please
          don't let me stop you from starting
          yours.

Anna turns and exits.

Christy looks down at Scott.

Scott sits and looks up at Christy.

Christy walks out of the room.

A door CLOSES.

INT. APARTMENT

MUSICAL MONTAGE

If possible, LED ZEPPELIN'S "DAZED AND CONFUSED"

CROSS CUT BETWEEN STUDIO AND BEDROOM

- Scott stares at a blank canvas.

- Anna puts on make-up - eye liner, eye shadow, lip gloss.

- Scott paces.

- Anna puts on stockings.

- Scott pours himself a drink.

- Anna puts on a bra. [Seen from behind] NO NUDITY

- Scott stands in front of the canvas with a pencil and makes marks. He doesn't like anything he draws.

- Anna puts on a nice form fitting dress.

- Scott lights a joint.

- Anna puts on high heels or knee high boots.

- Anna checks her phone notification. Her Uber has arrived.

- Anna walks out the door.

- Scott goes crazy, again. He breaks brushes. Smashes a glass.

- Scott throws out all of his paint but white.

- He begins splattering white paint on the canvas.

- He sits down as stares at his work.

- Scott stands and begins working the paint on the canvas.

- Scott pours white paint onto his palette.

- Broad stroke cover entire canvas.

- Spent, Scott steps back and studies his work. He smiles.

INT. APARTMENT - LATE NIGHT

Anna enters the apartment.

Scott sits on the sofa. He waited up for her come home.

He reaches for her.

She takes his hand and he leads her into the studio.

INT. APARTMENT - STUDIO - CONTINUOUS

Scott leads Anna to the canvas he painted.

Anna stands in front of it and admires it.

> ANNA
> Are you happy?

> SCOTT
> Finally.

> ANNA
> Good.

> SCOTT
> But...

> ANNA
> (frustrated)
> Scott, I think this is fine work --

> SCOTT
> I'm only happy if you're staying. I
> need you. You know that. I don't
> know why you stay, but I do know
> why I need you to stay.

Anna takes Scott's hand. They hug.

> ANNA
> I stay because the guilt of knowing
> you would be wallowing in self-pity
> would eat me alive the rest of my
> life.

Anna smiles.

                    SCOTT
          Nice.

Anna kisses him. She points at Scott and the canvas.

                    ANNA
          I stay because when you and this
          are connected, it's magical and you
          make me feel part of it.

INT. ART GALLERY - NIGHT

A well lit gallery.

TRACKING SHOT beginning with ECU of white paint on canvas.

[IF POSSIBLE "BITTERSWEET SYMPHONY" BY THE VERVE.]

                    SCOTT (V.O.)
          Life. Relationships. Painting. It's
          all art in one form or another. I
          need art to live. I need my
          relationships to create art. There
          is no right or wrong. There is no
          one way. Art is what art is. That
          may seem flippant but I am not
          trying to be. How can there be
          rules to what is boundless? Some
          argue for art for art sake, others
          call bullshit, and demand that art
          have meaning: context, subtext. Not
          even artists can agree on what art
          is so how can the general public be
          considered to know? This led to the
          rise of an evil called, critics --
          self appointed goose-steppers who
          prefer to pontificate on the
          importance of art purely out of
          self-preservation and to create a
          market that arbitrarily sets value
          on the artistic creations of
          others. If society just agreed to
          allow art to be what art wants to
          be, then we wouldn't need anyone to
          tell us what art is, let alone make
          a judgement of what good art is.
          Art doesn't give a shit!

                                        FADE TO WHITE:

www.ingramcontent.com/pod-product-compliance
Lightning Source LLC
Chambersburg PA
CBHW062101090426
42741CB00015B/3296